The Forgotten Promise:
Rejoining Our Cosmic Family

by Sherry Wilde

OZARK
MOUNTAIN
PUBLISHING

Library of Congress Cataloging-in-Publication Data

Wilde, Sherry-1950

The Forgotten Promise: Rejoining Our Cosmic Family by Sherry Wilde

A story of lifelong interaction with beings from another world.

1. UFO's 2. Abductions 3. Hypnosis 4. Extraterrestrials

1. Wilde, Sherry, 1950 II. UFO's III. The Forgotten Promise – Rejoining our Cosmic Family

Library of Congress Catalog Card Number: 2013952012

ISBN: 978-1-886940-48-2

Cover Design: enki3d.com

Book set in: Times New Roman

Book Design: Tab Pillar

Published by:

OZARK
MOUNTAIN
PUBLISHING

PO Box 754

Huntsville, AR 72740

800-935-0045 or 479-738-2348 fax: 479-738-2448

WWW.OZARKMT.COM

Printed in the United States of America

This is the story of one woman's lifelong interaction with beings from another world and her journey to go beyond the fear to find meaning and purpose.

In this book she explores the abduction experience and shares with you the Three Important Things they insisted she learn.

For Marion
I hope you found the answers.

For Vicky
For never—not once—doubting me.

And for Wanda
my port in a storm,
my guiding light,
my wise and knowing sister
I love you beyond words!

Table of Contents

Introduction

This is my story. I cannot prove any of what you are about to read but neither do I feel the need to convince you of its validity. It will either resonate with you, or it will not. For years I was encouraged to write about these experiences, but I resisted. It never felt right to make public such a personal and highly controversial episode from my life. For some reason, however, it suddenly became clear to me that now was the time to bring it out of the closet.

This is not an easy story for me to write, and it might not be easy for you to read or believe. I understand that. It will not be told in chronological order but will be told much in the same way as if I was sitting and visiting with you over a cup of coffee. A timeline has been added at the back of the book for you to reference if needed.

I want to emphasis that it is my story, and I've done my very best to keep others out of it—that is, family and friends who were peripherally involved—but it is impossible to tell the truth about what happened without including some facts about others' involvement. I did my level best to keep those parts to a minimum, especially those involving my children.

One of the first things I am asked after talking with others about this phenomenon is "Why you? What's so special about you?"

My answer is simple: Nothing. There is truly nothing special about me or my family. It is my belief that most of the people in this world have had at least one encounter with a being from another dimension or planet. Personally, I find it easier to think of them as coming from another dimension. Even though the beings I interacted with appeared to be transported here in a spaceship of some sort, I don't believe that distinction is worth exploring.

If you are drawn to this book, then it may very well be that you have had an inter-dimensional encounter, but the memory of that encounter is shielded from your consciousness for your own sanity. Trying to integrate these kinds of events into your life and still live what the world would consider a "normal" life is pretty much impossible. Even if you come to terms with what is happening to you, there is always the looming question of why. It is the reason so many alleged abductees are drawn to a path that takes them on a spiritual journey.

This book is not only a recounting of my experiences but also the story of how I discovered that, like most things, it is possible to turn the worst thing in your life into something positive just by choosing to look at it from a different perspective.

Prologue: It Starts with One

Backyard Abduction—1958—Rural Wisconsin

I couldn't have been more than eight years old. My younger brother and I were out behind our house playing on the sandstone rocks. My parents told me years later that they'd made a conscious decision to keep us somewhat isolated and protected from mainstream society—and we certainly were. It was the mid-1950s, and it was an altogether different world than it is now. We lived on a 120-acre non-working dairy farm that had a half-mile-long driveway off a little gravel road. We were a twenty-minute drive from the nearest village, and I attended a one-room schoolhouse until fourth grade at which time I underwent the traumatizing experience of being transferred into "town school."

It was an idyllic life. I had three siblings: a brother two years older than me, another brother one year younger, and my baby sister who came along when I was five. We were pushed out the door every summer morning and not allowed back into the house until lunch, and then out the door we would go again until dark. We ran the hills, played in the haymow, made forts, climbed trees, and splashed in the creek that ran through our valley farm. In the winter, we were bundled up and sent out the door to walk the three miles to school. (Yes, it actually was three miles.)

I remember my mother's warning, "Do not, no matter how tired you get, stop and lay down in the snow to sleep. You will freeze and never wake up!"

My father wasn't a farmer. He tried, but it just wasn't his calling. Instead, he went to work as a Greyhound bus driver. He was gone a lot.

3

Behind our house was a fence line that stretched all the way down the valley to our nearest neighbor. We could barely see their place from our upstairs window. My mother's garden was out there, and if we didn't stay out of her way, she'd put us to work pulling weeds, so we would disappear into the hills that surrounded our home. On this hot summer day, my younger brother and I were out behind the garden playing on the flat sandstone rocks. A fine assortment of berries grew wild in that area, and every now and then we'd break from our play long enough to go grab a handful.

My older brother was not with us, which was typical. He liked to go off by himself, fishing or exploring in the woods. I was standing in the tall grass, facing the gooseberry bush that grew along the fence, picking the berries and popping them into my mouth. The crisp sour taste of the berry was not my favorite, but I loved to make them pop and feel my mouth water as it reacted to the strong flavor.(I remember all of this as if it were yesterday.)

It was very hot and humid—almost claustrophobic. The buzzing of the insects was very loud in my ears and added to the feeling of closeness. There was no breeze, and I swatted away the mosquitos as they came close to my face or landed on my arms. I was focused on getting as many gooseberries into my mouth in as short a time as possible since I wanted to get back to my brother who was waiting over in the shade on the rocks.

I was plucking away with both hands, quickly picking a berry, popping it into my mouth, and going for the next one. Both hands were moving quickly over the bush, taking the easiest and ripest berries.

Suddenly, there was a change in the temperature. The hot stifling air, which only a moment before had felt as if it was going to suffocate me, turned noticeably cooler and the loud buzzing abruptly stopped. There was dead silence. I froze. The hair on the back of my neck stood up as a chill ran down my spine. I knew someone was standing behind me.

My heart was beating loudly in my chest as I slowly started to turn around. Strong hands came down on my shoulders and stopped me from moving. A gentle voice said my name and warned me not to turn around—as if I could with his hands firmly keeping me in place.

My mind raced as I tried to figure out who this could be. *An uncle? A neighbor?* And then a terrifying thought—*a stranger?*

But he had said my name. And his voice was somewhat familiar to me. There wasn't much time to consider all this because he started to talk to me in that same gentle tone. It calmed me a lot to hear that voice.

"What are you doing?" he said.

"Picking gooseberries," I replied.

"Why?"

"To eat," I said in a barely audible voice.

"What do they taste like?"

"Kinda sour," I whispered.

"Do you like them?" he asked.

"No."

He chuckled and said, "Then why are you eating them?"

"Because . . . why can't I turn around?" I pleaded.

"I think it would scare you to see me. Do you remember?"

Artist: Helen Endres

And I softly answered, "Yes."

After a moment he said, "Slowly turn around. Take hold of my hand and walk with me."

I instinctively kept my eyes averted as I turned and took hold of his hand. As we started to walk, I saw out of the corner of my eyes, three or four other beings, standing as if at attention among the tall

5

grass and shrubs. They didn't look real to me; they looked like the mannequins I'd seen at the JCPenney store, only they didn't seem to have human features. I tried getting a closer look but couldn't focus on their faces. I did notice, however, how small they were for being men. They were about my size and wore matching outfits that looked somewhat like the one-piece coveralls my dad wore in the winter, only these outfits were very tight and form fitting. They didn't appear to move or blink. They just stood there without moving a muscle.

Then I noticed my brother standing as if frozen over on the sandstone rocks. I asked if he could come with us but was told "Not now."

I glanced back at him again as we marched up the hill. I was afraid for my brother; he didn't look natural.

"What's wrong with my brother? Is he okay?"

"He is fine. He will be here when we return."

I trudged alongside my companion without fear. He seemed familiar to me, and the initial panic I'd felt was forgotten. I now turned to look ahead of me and saw for the first time our destination.

My heart started to pound as I looked up at a very shiny silver spaceship hovering up against the hillside. One side of it almost touched the steep terrain while the other was high up off the ground.

Now this was the mid to late 1950s, and I'd never seen a movie or TV show depicting a flying saucer, so this craft was fascinating for me to see. I'd seen planes flying overhead, and I'd been mesmerized by them moving through the sky, but this was different. It hung silently in the air without any support or wings. Glimmering in the sunlight, it hurt my eyes to look at it, and I squinted.

There were two more of the strange-looking little guys standing below it. Once again, I tried to look closely at their faces, and this time I was able to see two large black eyes. I was so spellbound by those big bug-like eyes that I really didn't take in any of their other features.

My companion walked with me under the ship, and standing behind me, he placed his hands on my shoulders as together we were lifted up through the air into the craft. How, I never understood. We simply floated up in a blue light.

They took me high above the earth. This memory is one I've had my whole life. It's a very strange thing, but I never questioned the reality of it, and yet if you would have asked me the next day or at any point during my childhood or early adult years if I'd ever seen a UFO or had an encounter, I would have answered "No."

It was kept in a separate place in my mind. I don't know how else to describe it. I was allowed to have this memory—they didn't want it buried. Otherwise, it certainly would have been put deep within the recesses of my mind—just like all the other encounters. But this one was different. This one contained a message they didn't want me to forget.

I remember very clearly standing with the grey alien I now refer to as "Da." There were a few others there with us as we stood looking out a large window. We were in outer space. There was blackness all around us and brilliant specks of stars scattered like seeds everywhere. It was spectacular. We were looking down at the amazing blue marble they told me was the earth.

I was only eight years old, but I could appreciate the enormity of what I was seeing. I was speechless for some time, and we all stood together in reverent silence. I moved closer to a large picture window and pressed my face up against it as I looked out, up, and down. In every direction I peered, there was darkness and deep silence.

We seemed to not be moving. We were suspended in space, and I was awestruck by the magnitude of what I was witnessing. Then I turned to Da and asked why the sky was black. *Was it now nighttime?*

An explanation was given in terms a young child could understand, and then Da said he wanted to show me something. The ship suddenly dropped down close to the blue globe that was my home, and we hovered above the Pacific Ocean. I was very young and certainly had not studied much geography, but somehow I comprehended what I was looking at.

We were high enough that I could see about half of the continental USA. Suddenly a wall of water rose up out of the ocean and moved toward the western coast of America. It quickly engulfed the land. Huge, black, billowing smoke clouds rose up along a newly formed coastline and continued to pop up randomly, going deeper and deeper into the continent. The whole western shoreline was gone as were the cities that had been there just moments before. Some of the water receded, but much remained while the fires continued to spread quickly over the dry land. Soon the earth was shrouded in black smoke. My beautiful blue planet was gritty and black. The world was on fire.

I started to cry.

Was my family dead?

"You did this! Why did you do this?"

I was angry and scared.

Was this spaceship now going to be my home? Would I never see my family again?

Da put his hands on my shoulders and looked deep into my eyes as he spoke softly but firmly. "This is the future. It hasn't happened—yet. And it doesn't have to happen, but it will if you humans don't change your ways."

I returned his gaze and tried to comprehend what he had just told me. I didn't understand what he meant by any of it.

Why show me this? Did he mean I was supposed to somehow change the course of events so this would not happen?

There was nothing I could do. It was outrageous to have put this on me. I felt angry and so helpless. It was too much. I was sobbing hard as I looked at him and tried to make him understand.

"But I'm just a little girl. What am I supposed to do?"

Keeping his hands on my shoulders while looking intensely into my eyes, he answered softly, "It starts with one."

We don't live in a world of reality;
we live in a world of perceptions.

Gerald J. Simmons

CHAPTER ONE:
Losing Normal

Decide to Undergo Hypnosis—Spring 1988

It was the spring of 1988 when I underwent hypnosis and finally filled in the blanks on a lifetime of partial memories. These memories, buried deep within the recesses of my mind, were of alien encounters. Prior to the regression, I'd been living the typical small town life of a 37-year-old working mother, wife, and co-owner of a small but successful real estate business in rural Wisconsin. I had absolutely no knowledge of the abduction experience. I knew, of course, that there were reports of UFO sightings from time to time, but I'd never read or heard anything about a person being taken aboard a craft by the occupants. I was more naïve about this kind of phenomenon than most, which is a fact I later came to know and understand.

That was the year I decided to undergo hypnosis in order to retrieve memories of a seemingly random act of aggression that had been inflicted on me by roadside workers—only the roadside workers turned out to be a race of extraterrestrials known as the "Greys." That in itself was more than I felt capable of coming to terms with, but what made this whole episode in my life so terribly hard to deal with was the horrible realization that not only had I been abducted by aliens during that incident, but I'd also had multiple abductions throughout my entire life.

There had been an enormous amount of activity beginning at a very early age. These beings had been a constant in my life but had somehow been able to bury the memories and keep me from having any conscious recall of the incidents. That frightened me and caused me a great deal of anguish. This was a lot to try to cope with, but then it got worse—way worse. I began having abduction experiences even as I was trying to come to terms with the memories that were flooding into my awareness. Suddenly I was experiencing encounters with them, and while not having total conscious recall, I would retain just enough to know it was happening. They were showing up sometimes three and four times in one week but then would be gone for a week or two. This activity went on for about two years. This is the story of my life during that period of time and the sacred lessons I learned once I was able to move past my fear.

After I underwent hypnosis and awakened to the memory of my abduction, I walked around in a stupor, barely able to function. The people who did the investigation of my encounters had me evaluated by a psychologist who was doing a study on the UFO abduction phenomenon, and I awaited the results of this evaluation with much hope. I was absolutely certain I would be found insane. This evaluation was done soon after my hypnosis, and I still had not integrated these experiences into my reality. I simply could not accept that this could happen. The present day abductions had not yet started, and all I was dealing with at that time were the memories. I'd convinced myself that it was all a mistake, a psychological anomaly that would be explained away by the right doctor and the right diagnosis.

So I headed off to the meeting with my investigator and the psychologist with an uplifted heart, certain of what I was going to hear. I was prepared to start whatever treatment was recommended. I was dumbfounded and crushed when my investigator told me that the overall test results came out very well. He stated that if it were possible to cheat on this test, they would consider that a possibility, as the results were that good. He seemed very pleased to be telling me this. I stood there, fighting back tears and fear as I realized the implications of what he was saying.

Not knowing how to deal with my reaction, he led me over to the psychologist who'd done the evaluation and let him speak to me. This doctor told me the test results were quite normal and did not indicate any pathology. I remember him saying there was a small elevation on the measure of paranoia, but they considered that normal, and they actually would have found it strange had I not shown some paranoia, given the experiences I was dealing with at the time. He went on to say that one of the tests, a test on fantasy proneness, indicated I was no more prone to fabrication than anyone else.

My investigator was confused by my reaction to this; he had expected relief from me, even happiness. He didn't understand how badly I'd wanted a diagnosis—I had been counting on a diagnosis. Something they could treat with therapy or a pill—I didn't care. At that time, anything would have been better than being told that what had happened to me was real.

After that, I went off to visit three or four other respected psychologists in order to find one that would get it right. None did. They all agreed that mentally, I appeared to be sound. Where the problem existed, according to each and every one of them, was in our interpretation of the world or what we perceived to be normal in our world. That blew me away.

As I told a psychologist who tried to help me, "It's like I have this box of memories—they are from my life—I can't deny that. But where do I put this box of memories? I put it on the shelf in my mind that is marked *fiction/fantasy* (which is where I really, really want it to go), but it gets bumped back off into my arms. Doesn't belong there. I try putting it on the *dream* shelf, but off it comes. Doesn't belong there either. So I try to put it on the shelf marked *real life experiences*, but I can't leave it there. I cannot accept that it belongs there. Because if it belongs there, then everything I thought I knew about life—not just *my* life but *life*—is a lie."

And so began a journey to discover the answer to the age-old question: "What's it all about?"

Actually, I'd been a bit of a seeker even before these memories came to the forefront of my mind—probably because these encounters started at an early age. As best I can figure, these beings were a presence in my life by the age of five, and I would guess even long before that. Just as they dictated the exact moment of my daughter's conception, I believe they had a hand in mine. It is not just the act of discovering that you have been abducted by beings from another world that sets you off on the road to self-discovery, but it's also the things they teach you. I was given lessons right from the beginning, and I was expected to learn them.

So Many Lessons

"What is the most important thing to know?" they would ask over and over again.

And each time they would go deeper and deeper into the meaning of the lesson. They taught me a lot over the years, and their subjects ranged from the complexities of life to the mechanics and operations of their crafts. Things like how their ships can go from one end of the galaxy to the other, how the ships fly so quietly, how they can walk through walls, and more importantly, how they can pull me right through those same seemingly solid walls. They taught me how easy it is to heal our body and showed me that the power of our minds was beyond anything we could imagine. They explained why two people can be standing side by side, and one sees a UFO and the other person remains totally oblivious. They proved to me that time does not exist. They taught me about vibration and the light that is within us all. Among other things, they told me where they came from and why they were here. And they drilled into me "The Three Important Things to Know."

Many investigators and abductees believe my captors are evil, but I don't necessarily share that opinion. They are known in ufology as the Greys, and it's true that most of the time they did appear to be ruthless and callous. I do believe it is all about perception—much like a young child would perceive a doctor to be mean when he sticks him with a needle in order to administer a vaccination. One thing, however, is for certain— they have a wicked sense of humor. There is an indifference that is demonstrated that will make them seem extremely cruel, but then they will suddenly turn around and show deep compassion and love.

It took a lot of looking at their behavior to recognize that I had to step outside of the experience and let go of my perceptions—the filters I was running it all through—so that I could view it from a more detached angle in order to get clarity. That was a huge part of my coming to terms with these experiences. It enabled me to see it as an observer rather than as the victim.

How could evil beings teach what they were teaching? That didn't make any sense to me. They always insisted I learn certain things, and they tested me over and over again on The Three Important Things to Know. If I have any regrets about these visitors to my life, it is that I failed to learn all the knowledge they were willing to impart.

The Paradox of UFO Abductions

That is the paradox. The UFO abduction experiences are very difficult to unravel due to their very nature. Really, what exactly are we talking about here? Little grey inimical men coming into your house—through your walls, no less—and pulling you from your bed after putting you into an altered state of consciousness. Taking you back through those same seemingly solid walls to a silver spaceship parked on your side lawn for all the neighbors to see. Taking you aboard the ship and in many instances violating you and returning you to your bed. All this outrageousness, and you're left with no memory and no witnesses?

Right. Why would anyone doubt that story?

One of the reasons I have no interest in trying to convince you of the reality of these events is simply because I cannot. What proof do I have to offer you? None. Do you think I don't see the absurdity of it? I don't have issues with anyone that doesn't buy into this, not one bit. But I do think it is shortsighted of people to pass judgment on something they have no firsthand knowledge of. To show such a lack of compassion for those whose lives have been torn to shreds over the complete and utter helplessness experienced by the seemingly unwilling participants of this phenomenon is brutally cold. I do not use the word "victim" to describe those of us who have been abducted, or if you prefer, those of us who *believe* we've been abducted. I can only speak for myself on this issue, but I refuse to buy into the victim mindset.

It was not always so. Initially, I did believe I was being victimized. It took a whole lot of work to get to a place where I truly could know on a very deep level that they were not the perpetrators and I the victim. That was a huge step in the healing process, and it was a critical point in allowing a shift in perception to take place. I now realize that no one is a victim, and I don't care what the situation is. That is the point I had to take myself to before I could even begin to function somewhat normally. You don't get there overnight. The world teaches us that there are perpetrators and there are victims. It's everywhere: in our media, our churches, our corporations, our government, our schools, and our families.

Moving beyond fear and into acceptance of the experience was the hardest. My mind kept rejecting it, even in the face of mounting evidence. And understandably so. We have a coping mechanism built into who we are—a part of us that insists that everything make sense and be understood within the confines of what we know to be true and that truth is predicated on our prior experiences in this life. We trust in our five senses because they have served us well.

We know intellectually that solid objects are not as they appear, and that includes our bodies. Scientists tell us we are 99.9% space—non-matter. But accepting the concept that we can walk through "solid" walls is beyond our abilities because it is not part of our experience. We don't believe it, we don't trust it, and so it is not possible. Our minds reject it. So, even if you saw someone walk through a wall, your mind is going to find a way to make it into lie. A trick.

And so it is with the UFO experiences. They don't fit into anything we perceive to be normal, so we reject the whole thing. Our mind is more than willing to help us find a way to rationalize away the episode by convincing us we were dreaming, hallucinating, or fantasizing. Those of us who have these experiences understand why it is so hard for the general public to believe our stories. After all, we lived through the experience, and we're having trouble believing it.

A friend once asked me if I ever knew ahead of time when these guys were going to show up. I replied that usually I did. I could "smell" them.

"Really, you can really smell them?" he asked.

"No," I answered, "I don't actually *smell* them, but there is a sense that I have, a sense that has no name, and that is the best way for me to state it."

How do you describe something to another that is unexplainable even to yourself? There was always a part of me that was tuned in to them—a part of me that knew them and was in sync with them. During that period of time, when they were so involved in my life, I was bewildered and confused about how I could "feel" them or as stated earlier "smell" them. It was one of the issues I had the most trouble coming to terms with. At that time, I didn't understand what my connection to them was, but I did know that they had influenced my development more than anyone or anything else.

I faltered many times along the way during that period of time as I struggled to incorporate all that I was remembering, plus all that I was experiencing, into a life that I could face on a day to day basis. It was so very hard to come to terms with what I was discovering about myself and the seemingly "secret life" I had been living without conscious memory that it caused me to question everything.

Over and over again, I would recount the memories, and for a long period of time my mind would search to find rational explanations until eventually the evidence was so overwhelming that I had to accept the reality of the experience, but even then I continued to look for an explanation that made sense. Eventually, it was the very teachings of my abductors that gave way to the insights that allowed me to understand that nothing really happens to us without our consent, at least on some level.

Believe me, I tried very hard to keep the events I was witness to contained within my mind, thereby avoiding the physical reality of the encounters. Call it a dream, night paralysis, or an over active imagination—anything was better than accepting that these things were happening in real time and real life—but I could not leave it there in my imagination or dreams. This was not that easily explained away due to all the physical evidence to the contrary.

Too many times I would see the proof on my own body in the form of bruises, needle marks, and other physical scars. Sometimes I would find the grass in my side yard flattened in a swirling circular shape. Also, because so many of my encounters happened during times I was around others, missing time and other evidence of my experience would be supported by these witnesses. My objective searching and questioning of these activities in my life forced me to look at my existence from a higher perspective.

For the very sake of my survival, I had to understand why this was happening to me and how it could happen. Not *how* as in how did they walk through those walls but even deeper than that. How was this allowed to happen in a universe that I had always believed was governed by God? How was it possible that I was allowed to be some other race's "specimen" or guinea pig? Where was God in all this? I found my answers eventually, but for many years I was left feeling like the ultimate victim.

Soon after having the reservoir of my memories opened through hypnosis, I started to experience my encounters in what I think of as "real time." That is, I was aware of their presence, and I knew not only when they were nearby but pretty much when they were coming for me, so a lot of the things they were doing with me and teaching me were left in my conscious mind.

During this period of time the activity was staggering—and exhausting. I was literally living in two worlds. To survive the experiences, I was forced out of necessity to come to some sort of conclusion as to how and why this was happening.

One day I got a call from a lady I'd done some business with but didn't know on a personal level. She said that she'd heard the stories about the UFO activity going on around my house. My response was barely civil. I wasn't ready to talk to anyone outside the chosen few about any of this, and it upset me that people were talking. I had children and a business to think about. I knew just enough about this lady to know that she was a gentle-natured person and would never get confrontational with anyone, so I wondered why the hell she had called me to say such a thing.

I was evasive and made moves to get off the phone when I heard her say that she just wanted me to know that she believed the stories and didn't think I was a kook. That gave me pause. Here was a woman, willing to go on record as believing that what was happening to me was real when I wasn't even sure I could say the same thing. I heard the sincerity in her voice and decided to let her talk.

My Lifeline

She invited me to a meeting of a group of about a dozen people that got together every week to meditate and discuss life. I declined. That just wasn't my cup of tea, especially with all that was going on with me, but she was persistent. Her calm demeanor and sincerity eventually won me over, and I finally

17

relented and agreed to let her pick me up and take me to their gathering that evening.

I look back all these years later, and I recognize that that lady was an angel. It's quite possible she saved my life. It was that group that became my lifeline and opened me up to a new way of looking at things. Struggling to deal with the bizarre nature of these experiences had left me scared and uncertain about everything. The UFO activity at my house was escalating, and I was in a state of near panic. My marriage was under tremendous strain, my children were being adversely affected, my business was suffering, and I had nowhere to turn for answers.

As we rode up to the meeting that night, I felt certain that it was going to be the same old thing I always encountered when people heard about my experiences. The questions were pretty much always the same: "How do they talk to you? What do they feel like? What do they do to you?"

I was wrong. Instead, no one seemed interested in the "nuts and bolts" of the abduction. They weren't interested at all in the "experience"; they seemed to be looking behind the abduction as if to find a higher purpose in the whole thing. It felt like balm for my soul. When the group broke for snacks, I stayed sitting on the sofa.

A very kind, calm man stayed where he was, and when we were alone in the room, he leaned toward me and asked in a very gentle voice, "So, how are you doing? How are you _really_ doing?"

I replied that above all else I was afraid—not just for me, but for my children.

He held my gaze as he said with all the certainty in the world, "You know there are no victims."

I stared at him for a good long while before replying that I certainly couldn't agree with that. "Look at the facts. I'm not in agreement with what is going on. That makes me a victim."

With so soft a voice I had to lean forward to hear him, he explained to me that we don't always see the big picture.

18

"How did I know that on some level at some time prior to my even coming into this world, I didn't agree to be a part of this experience?" I understood what he was saying, and Lord knows, I wanted to believe him, but it was so hard to fathom. I pondered his words for days, maybe weeks. I never forgot them and they became a lifeline for me—I played them over and over again. I clung to them during my worst moments. It took me years to integrate the true essence of that belief into my being, but with much guidance, inspiration, and help from unlikely places, I did.

Not everything that is faced can be changed,
but nothing can be changed until it is faced.

James Baldwin

CHAPTER TWO:
Unanswered Questions

Revisit After 20 Years—September 2010

One of my more conscious encounters with the Greys occurred in September of 2010. I had turned 60 years of age on Christmas Day of that same year. Because I knew it was unusual for them to stay involved in a woman's life past menopause since much of their interest seems to be centered on harvesting eggs, I asked what they were doing back here again. They seemed surprised at the question—almost insulted.

I'd long ago learned that there are different "levels" of these beings known as Greys. Primarily during a typical abduction experience, we come in contact with the two bottom tiers. There is what I think of as the "worker" Greys, and then there is the "lead guy" who is the one that communicates with you telepathically. His is the voice that is very well-known to me. Where the workers seldom show any emotion, rarely talk, and are quite cold toward you, the lead guy can demonstrate kindness, concern, and even love. He shows emotion, not just through his eyes, but also through his energy. This lead guy felt like my father, and he is the one I refer to as Da. More than once, I begged to stay with him and not be returned to the world where nothing seemed to make sense to me. You see, the love experienced in the old third-dimensional world seems pale and thin compared to what I experience with him.

Over the course of the past twenty years, I've worked hard to come to terms with these visitors from another world. One of the toughest things for me to explain is how I could feel such love from Da when with him and beg more often than not to stay with him—and yet be terrified of them when they showed up again in my life. It's hard to explain to you as I don't really have a clear understanding of it myself, but it might have to do with the visceral reaction that our physical self feels when confronted by something not of the norm.

There is a change of perception that takes place when you are in the higher vibration of these beings. There is a sense of righteousness, of order, and a purer understanding of our place in the cosmos. I know how contradictory that sounds, given that I was being treated like a lab rat during parts of these experiences, and I understand that it may be that I have been "brainwashed" or even programmed by them to believe this. Lord knows they were able to manipulate my behavior in so many ways.

As you read my story, you will see just how capable they are of controlling me and planting certain ideas or beliefs into my mind. But you see, I have chosen to believe that these beings are not malicious. I have looked at the evidence, and I have made my conclusion. I am open to hearing what others have to say, but for me I am comfortable with my analysis of them so far as they pertain to my life events. Maybe, just maybe, they don't look upon the body in the same way we do. It seems from what I gleaned from their teachings, that our bodies are just containers. Our true essence is so much more than that, and our bodies are not of significant value but more of a vehicle for us in this dimension. If that is the case, it would go a long way in explaining their often insensitive treatment of me and others who were participants in their program.

To truly understand them, I need to be totally without fear, which is a tall order to fill. My fear, while not totally alleviated, has been brought under control—for the most part. To me, their behavior is still erratic and not always easily understood, but I have come to a truce of sorts, as well as an acceptance of their involvement in my life. So when they returned after about a 20-year absence, I was relatively calm but surprised.

Local UFO Flap—January 1987

To fully understand the meaning of their latest visit, we need to go back and recount the events of the previous encounters. It was January of 1987 when a UFO flap occurred in my community, and everyone was talking about it. A UFO flap is defined as an inordinate number of people reporting sightings of unknown flying objects in the skies. This can include vague accounts of suspicious lights or actual sightings of what appear to be solid vehicles of an unknown origin.

There were dozens of these reports made in my area over a four-month period of time, so investigators came to town to interview people and see what was happening. I was barely aware of the hoopla surrounding these events. My life was focused on my two daughters and my career. All the memories of my alien encounters were still buried deep within my subconscious mind although right around this same time I started to become quite fixated on an event that had occurred years before. I'd started to replay it over and over again, trying to complete the memory and fill in the blanks. Every night before going to sleep, I went over the events of that day back in 1968 when I was seventeen years old. I thought if I could fall asleep thinking about it, my subconscious mind would bring the details to the surface.

Roadside Abduction (Partial Memories)

I'd been driving my little VW Beetle to my girlfriend's house located a good ten miles away from my home. I was meeting up with her and her sister to go shopping for the afternoon, and there was a deadline—I needed to be there by 10:00 a.m., or they'd leave without me! The winters in Wisconsin are brutal, but this spring day was a gift, all sunny and warm with the birds singing and life coming back to the trees and fields. I was feeling happy and carefree as you do when you're young; I was driving along with the window down and the radio turned up high. I wasn't driving fast. No need. I was going to make it right on time.

23

As I approached a small rise in the road, two things happened simultaneously. I noticed some men working alongside the road carrying sticks or wands of some sort. They were moving them over the ground in a sweeping motion, and at the same time, my car stalled. As my car rolled to a stop, I noticed one of the men had stepped out into the road and raised his hand. His eyes were very penetrating, and as he looked at me, it felt as if he was looking straight into my soul. I knew this, and yet I couldn't get a good fix on his face. I couldn't see him clearly, but I remembered those dark eyes looking in through the windshield at me.

My memory was blank after that—until I reached Vicky's house and walked in two hours late.

This event had happened twenty years ago, but now it seemed to come from out of nowhere, and it was weighing on me. I needed to remember his face! And why had I not tried harder before to remember what had happened to me during those two hours of missing time? Why had I just let this go? Suddenly, it was urgent that I remember. I had started to consider hypnosis as a way to finally get through whatever barrier was keeping me from accessing the memories of this event.

I always figured I'd been pulled from the car by those men in matching coveralls and sexually assaulted. Something had happened to me—something so terrible that my mind had shut out the memory. I noticed that whenever I was driving or riding along with someone, and we came up on a crew working alongside the road, I would start to panic. Sometimes I'd break into a cold sweat and my body would tremble. I'd have trouble breathing. The fear was that intense. But if I'd been attacked, why didn't I suffer any physical scars? I didn't recall any kind of trauma to my body from that day, and probably just as significant was the fact that I'd been a virgin when I married. Just what had happened to me alongside that quiet country road?

I didn't know why this particular memory was starting to plague me, but it was there every night as I went to sleep.

Looking back, I realize the significance of the timing, but back then it seemed like a random thought that appeared to get stuck in my head.

So in January of 1987 while the local UFO flap was making news around the world, I was only vaguely aware of it and had virtually no interest in it. I had absolutely no reason to connect my latest obsession with the lost time I'd experienced back in the '60s with a UFO encounter. When my long-time friend, Vicky, called and asked me to attend the informational meeting the investigators were holding, I declined. It wasn't something that piqued my interest. Then she brought up the lost-time incident that I'd experienced while on my way to her house to go shopping. The very same incident I'd recently started to obsess over.

Vicky's Perspective of the Roadside Incident

I listened closely as she told me her perspective of that day. She recalled that I'd come racing into her house two hours late, talking about seeing little men—aliens—and being on a spaceship. She insisted that I had tried to convince her to go back with me to see them.

"Didn't I remember?"

What the hell was she talking about? I think I would have remembered saying such things.

She said that my "missing time" might be linked to a UFO encounter of some sort. Then she went on to remind me of a few other strange occurrences that she'd been witness to in our teen years when we'd been inseparable.

As I listened to her, I was shocked. She was right! There had been some pretty strange incidents that I'd just let go of or swept under the rug.

How could I have done that? Such significant, bizarre things! What was wrong with me that I would do such a thing? It wasn't normal.

My Mother's Memories of That Timeframe

I mentioned the conversation I had with Vicky to my mother, and she added to my misery by reminding me that she remembered that particular time in my life. She recalled me talking about seeing a flying saucer, as well as claiming to have had an encounter with spacemen.

She said that I'd always had an obsession with drawing the face of what we would all now recognize as a Grey. That was true. If you look back in the workbooks she'd saved from grammar school, there were faces of what I now recognize to be aliens drawn in the margins.

Growing Discomfort

This was getting more and more uncomfortable. I decided I needed to look further into what was going on in my own backyard. I read a few newspaper articles about the UFO reports and talked to a couple of the local people. I discovered that there had been witness reports of "missing time." That is, people who had seen a UFO had reported that a block of time was unaccounted for; they were missing an hour or so with no memory of what had occurred.

CUFOS' Briefing

The word was that the investigators would use hypnosis in order to help these people retrieve their lost memories. This was of interest to me for obvious reasons—hadn't I just recently decided to undergo hypnosis myself in an effort to uncover my own lost memories from the roadside incident?

I decided to attend the informational meeting with Vicky, just to satisfy my curiosity and see what I could learn. I figured these people might be able to recommend a good hypnotist, as I didn't want to just pick anybody at random out of the yellow pages. So I did a complete reversal and told Vicky I'd go with her to the meeting. My incentive was to get the name of a reputable hypnotist. The idea that I might have had any kind of UFO contact was still not even plausible to me.

The gymnasium was pretty much abuzz with the local people who'd come to hear about the strange lights they were seeing in the sky. I was indifferent and feeling a little bit defensive about the whole thing. I didn't particularly like the idea of beings from another planet visiting our earth. It was a scary concept, and I was prepared to find lots of holes in anyone's argument that it was possible. To say I was skeptical would be an understatement.

The investigators were from CUFOS—the J. Allan Hynek Center for UFO Studies out of Chicago. They did a good job of keeping it balanced and didn't try to convince us that what the local people were seeing in the skies were truly alien spacecraft.

Well, that was a relief.

They went on to say that several people had approached them to report sightings, and many of the witnesses were credible and some sightings were supported by other witnesses.

Okay, I could live with that.

Something was up there buzzing around, but that didn't mean it was a spaceship from another planet for heaven's sake! Gently they moved the discussion to lost time and the possible implications.

Now they were starting to tread on thin ice. They were actually implying that some of us sitting there in that audience could have been picked up by creatures from outer space and taken aboard a craft—against our will!

No way. They'd gone too far. I was ready to leave.

I was making moves to go when they showed some pictures of the types of crafts that had been reported in the skies around our community. My heart stalled—then it started to pound. I felt faint. I wanted to run from the room.

Flashback of White Globe Sighting

How could I have forgotten?

My brain became overloaded with memories. They rushed at me like a movie in fast forward. They had shown a picture of a big white globe with orange lights, and it was exactly what I'd seen in the sky just a few nights earlier.

What was wrong with me?

How can a person see a big other-worldly craft like that in the sky and not remember? Not only did I see it, but other memories flooded over me.

Think—slow down—put it in sequence. How did it go? I struggled to bring it to the surface.

Oh yeah, I'd gone to show a property I had listed out in the country. It was located about twenty minutes north of town. My appointment was set for 5:00 p.m., but the buyer never showed.

Finally after waiting thirty minutes, I gave up and started the drive back to town. I was headed south down the long hill that brought me into the valley where our village was located when suddenly ahead of me and to the right, I saw a very large round craft of some sort.

I tried to make sense of it. It appeared to be more than twice the size of a full moon, and it was solid white with red-orange lights blinking on it. I glanced over toward the sun and noted that it was still quite high above the horizon, so there was no mistaking this globe for it. Besides, this object definitely seemed very mechanical. It was just hanging there in the sky, and as I watched it, I could see it was moving very, very slowly toward the east.

It was bizarre, and I had a hard time keeping my eyes off it as I drove the last few miles into town. I didn't want to turn off toward my home and lose sight of it, so I kept driving toward it. Soon I was on the southern edge of the village, and the craft was looming large in the sky. I was afraid to go any closer, so I pulled into the gas station, thinking I could watch it and talk to the other people there about it.

I remember thinking *There is safety in numbers!*

This part was strange. There were several cars parked at the pumps, but not one person was looking at that big odd thing hanging in the sky. It was unfathomable to me that nobody else could see it. It was just too obvious!

I looked around for someone to notice, but nobody did, so then I looked for someone I would recognize so I could speak to them and point it out, but there was not one familiar face there. I slowly topped off my tank with gas—all the while watching the sphere in the sky.

Then I walked into the convenience store to pay for it. I was a regular at this station and knew, if not by name, then at least by recognition, most all the clerks. The moment I walked into that store I knew something was off. It buzzed like a beehive and the people in there were oddly short in stature and moved in quick, jerky motions. I didn't know a soul. I quickly paid and left.

Lost Time

When I walked out, the first thing I noticed was that it had gotten strangely dark out during the short period of time I'd been in the store. I turned to look for the big white globe, but it was gone. Relieved, I headed off on the quick five-minute drive home.

I pulled into my driveway and noticed my husband and youngest daughter out in the front yard. They seemed agitated and excited. My daughter came running over to the car and explained that they'd had a "flying saucer" over the house just a little while ago. My husband confirmed this bit of news.

Strangely, I'd forgotten all about my sighting and never mentioned it. Furthermore, I wasn't all that interested in what they were telling me. I went into the house and immediately noticed that it was almost 7:30 p.m. That got my attention.

It didn't make any sense. I went over and over the events of the evening. At 5:00 I was at the property. I had left at 5:30 and made the 20-minute drive back to the village. Even if I allowed 30 minutes for the drive back to town, that would put it at 6:00 when I got to the gas station. It should be no later than 6:20. It was 7:30. I was missing over an hour of my life.

I became quite troubled and upset about this, but oddly enough, that concern also left my awareness before long. That is, until now.

Only Seeking the Name of a Good Hypnotist

I sat there stunned and fearful. I turned to Vicky and told her about the sighting I'd had just a few nights ago but had somehow forgotten. I was seriously scared. It made no sense to me that I could have had such an experience and totally forgotten it. Vicky urged me to go talk to one of the people from CUFOS and tell them about this sighting and the story of my lost time experience back when I was a teenager.

The speakers had just asked that anyone who'd seen something odd in the sky to please come forward. I decided to take Vicky's advice and go up to speak with them about my sighting, but I wasn't sure about sharing my roadside story from the '60s since I couldn't see that it had anything to do with UFOs.

What I really wanted out of this meeting was the name of a good hypnotist. That's all. I knew enough to know that hypnosis was not something to be entered into lightly, especially when you don't know what memory you're going to unlock. So away I went to find one of the speakers.

Meeting Don

I felt pretty silly going up to Don Schmitt and introducing myself. I knew he was there to investigate some serious stuff, and I didn't have much to offer him other than the white globe sighting I'd had recently. He listened to my account and asked a few questions. Then he asked that I go give that information to the other fellow there.

I never did tell him what had happened at the gas station or that my husband and daughter had seen a silver ship over our house around the same time I was seeing the white globe. I never told him about the missing time—it just didn't occur to me. Also, I didn't really care much about all that. I had one thing on my mind, and that was to get the name of a good hypnotist.

Finally, I got up the nerve to ask him. He inquired as to why I wanted a hypnotist, and I gave him a much abbreviated version of what had happened on my way to Vicky's house back in the late '60s. He was very patient in listening to my story, but I felt the fool and was regretting my decision to bother him. He seemed more interested in this story than the white globe story.

That didn't make sense to me. He was asking probing, pointed questions about the roadside experience. I couldn't understand why. I explained to him that nothing having to do with UFOs had occurred back then, and he seemed to accept that. He said he wanted to speak with me further about using hypnosis as a way to unlock those memories.

We exchanged contact information and agreed to talk again in the next week or so. I walked away sure that there would be no further contact from Mr. Schmitt.

To my surprise, he called me within the two weeks just like he said he would. The conversation evolved around the events of that day so long ago when my car had stalled on the way to Vicky's house. I never for a minute thought alien abduction was a possibility for me or anyone else. It didn't register in my brain as something that could really happen.

I thought it strange that a man who appeared to be rational and educated could subscribe to such nonsense, but in the end, I didn't care. I just wanted to secure a hypnosis session that would be structured and safe in order to get to the bottom of my lost time episode.

Don offered to help me try to put the pieces of that experience together, but I was confused by his offer. This was no UFO experience. This had been workmen who had somehow stopped my car and done something so terrible to me that I'd hidden the event deep within my mind. I needed to know what had happened! I needed to undergo hypnosis! But Don was not at all convinced that hypnosis was a good idea.

As a matter of fact, he was pretty much against it. My response was that I would find a hypnotist and pursue the lost memory on my own since I was sure aliens had nothing to do with it anyway. He stated that hypnosis was not a good investigative tool as retrieving repressed memories was serious business and should not be taken lightly. He explained that while under hypnosis, individuals are extremely vulnerable to suggestion and only a highly qualified person should ever attempt to retrieve memories, especially potentially traumatic ones.

That made sense, but it raised new questions for me. If I did undergo hypnosis, and it started out with the premise that I'd been abducted by aliens, couldn't they "lead me" in that direction?

He assured me that the alien abduction experience is not one they go looking for. That would taint the investigation. Then Mr. Schmitt asked if I had ever done any reading on UFOs or the abduction phenomenon.

I replied that I had not; my father was the one in the family who had interest in that stuff. I'd given him a book about UFOs once at Christmas, but I hadn't even bothered to read it myself.

We ended our conversation but not before he convinced me to not seek hypnosis on my own. Well, I refused to commit to anything; it was just all so wacky.

In the end, it was decided that hypnosis would be used to explore the lost time I'd experienced when I was a teenager and that CUFOS would be involved. The facts of the case as presented, convinced Don to dig deeper into this episode. The incident happening in the middle of the day, having witnesses to the two hours of lost time along with my conscious memory of seeing four men standing by the side of the road, and the fact that my car had just died and rolled to a stop for no discernible reason all gave weight to his decision.

As for me, I'd become convinced that hypnosis was not something I wanted to pursue on my own. Talking with Don about it had made it more real, and I was feeling a bit vulnerable. I knew I would never find a hypnotist that came anywhere near to being the professional that they had access to, so I agreed to allow CUFOS to be involved.

If we all worked on the assumption that what is accepted as true were really true, there would be little hope of advance.

Orville Wright

Chapter 3:
Losing My Innocence

First Hypnosis Session—1988

My husband accompanied me on the trip to Chicago for the regression, and the whole thing had a surreal feel about it. I kept thinking about all the other things we could have been enjoying on this warm spring day.

What a silly, stupid thing to be doing—what was wrong with me! I thought.

We made our way to the CUFOS office where we met up with Don. I was feeling deeply embarrassed about this whole hullabaloo, and I couldn't stop myself from apologizing profusely to him as I warned him again and again that this was going to be a gigantic waste of everyone's time. I explained to him that all they were about to find stored deep in the recesses of my mind was a story of how some road workers had surrounded my car and somehow delayed me in getting to my destination. I was now sure that nothing of any significance had even happened to me on that day. Surprisingly, Don agreed with me, saying that no doubt that was the case and how relieved I would be to put this memory to rest.

We were waiting for another man to join us, and when he arrived, he and Don went into the next room and talked behind closed doors for some time. I paced the room and tried to figure out a way to get out of this mess. I even thought of bolting, but that would have made things even worse. I was a very private person, and all this attention to such a minor insignificant event in my life—an event that had happened twenty years ago—now felt terribly silly.

After a bit, Don and the other man who turned out to be a young psychologist who was doing a study on alien abductions came out, and we made our way to downtown Chicago and the office of Stanley V. Mitchell. Surprisingly, Mr. Mitchell was a UFO skeptic. He was the former President of the Association for Advanced Ethical Hypnotists, and his credentials were exemplary. Mr. Mitchell had helped develop a technique known as "battlefield hypnosis that was used during the Korean War to treat war injuries without the aid of anesthesia, and he was a pioneer in the use of hypnosis during open heart surgery. This guy was no "back alley" amateur; he was a serious, well-respected professional!

Oh my gosh! What a mess! How could I have gotten all these people involved in my obsession about this trivial little event in my life? I was regretting very much the ploy I'd undertaken just so I could finally find the answers to my lost-time episode.

Mr. Mitchell was very kind. He was a bit grandfatherly, and I trusted him immediately. He could see how nervous I was, and I couldn't stop myself from apologizing to him as well. I felt bad that he was stuck here in his office on a weekend, putting time into something that was going to amount to a hill of beans.

Mr. Mitchell explained hypnosis to me. It was not, as some believe, a deep state of sleep or unconsciousness where you are easily influenced to do or believe something that is not acceptable or true for you. Indeed, it was just the opposite. It was a heightened state of awareness where time didn't exist. In other words, I would be able to go back to that day when my car had stalled and "relive" the whole experience as if it were happening in real time. A part of me would be aware that I was sitting in his office in downtown Chicago while a larger part of my awareness would be back there, living the experience again. He would be there to remind me that I was safe.

When I felt ready, he proceeded to "put me under." It took him a considerable amount of time, and later, Don told me that they had almost given up. Still, I was astonished when he told me he was ready to take me back to that day. I explained that I was not yet under hypnosis. He countered that I was indeed under hypnosis, and to prove the point, he stuck a rather large needle into the palm of my hand after telling me it would not hurt. I looked at that needle sticking halfway through my hand and was convinced—because, true enough, there was no pain. It was, however, fascinating to me that I felt no different from when I'd been sitting there chatting with him ten minutes earlier. As a result, I was not expecting much from this process.

A Return to the Roadside Abduction Experience

He asked me to go back to the day that I'd been on my way to Vicky's house to go shopping with her and her sister. It took a little bit of effort, but eventually I found myself back there. It was amazing! I was in that little blue VW Bug, racing through the Wisconsin countryside.

Ahhhh, I could feel the warm spring air coming in through the open window, and I could hear the song on the radio. It was a Beach Boys song—a favorite group of mine. I was feeling happy, carefree, and like anything was possible! I was singing along with the radio, going about 58 mph along a straight stretch of road. I was only about five minutes from Vicky's house, and I was going to be right on time. They would be finished with chores and ready to leave when I got there. We were going shopping for school clothes, and I actually had some money to spend. Life was good.

As I raced along, the car engine suddenly stopped—just went dead for no reason. The car was rolling to a stop just as I became aware of some workers standing by the side of the road. They had some kind of wand or stick in their hands. *What were they doing waving those instruments at the ground?*

It struck me as a strange kind of job. It appeared they might be using metal detectors and were searching the ground for something. I noticed they were all dressed alike in blue-grey coveralls.

I had a quick thought: *Good thing my car stalled to slow me down because I might not have noticed them in time.*

One of the workers had stepped out into the road. The fool was standing in the middle of my lane. I'm trying to figure out who these guys are.

Workers? No. Maybe they are from the bow hunters club down the road? Maybe they lost an arrow, and that's what they're searching for in the ditch.

But even as I have that thought, I realize it doesn't make sense.

Bow hunters don't dress alike in coveralls, and we're a good quarter mile or more from the clubhouse.

The one man is walking toward me, and his eyes are hypnotic. Now my memory stalls. I can't seem to go any further. Over and over again Mr. Mitchell took me through the events leading up to this moment, and over and over again I would falter and could go no further. Finally after many attempts I broke through the block.

Under hypnosis, I lifted my right foot as I relived the experience of taking it off the accelerator, and my left foot made the motion of pushing down on the clutch. At the same time, my right hand moved over and reenacted the experience of turning off the radio. I intended to "pop the clutch" to get the car going again. It had no effect, so I reached over and turned the engine off and tried to restart it. It was dead, totally unresponsive.

By now, the car had rolled to a stop in front of the man standing in the road. I couldn't focus on him. It was like he was there, but I couldn't get a clear image of him.

Then he spoke, "Hello, Sherry. We've been waiting for you."

My mind reeled as I tried to comprehend and make sense of what I'd just heard.

Who was this person that knew my name and knew enough about me and my life to know I'd be driving down this road at this exact time?
I looked out through the windshield and was terrified to see that he was not human. I observed my mind trying to make changes to what I was seeing, trying to "correct" the vision that my eyes were showing me.

The other men who'd been working in the ditch with their wands were walking toward the car. Then the man who'd spoken leaned on the hood of my car with both hands and peered in through the windshield. I immediately looked away and somehow managed to roll my window up, lock the door, and grab the steering wheel with both hands. I put my head down on my arms up against the steering wheel and refused to look at him.

"It's Time," He Said.

He got very sharp with me and called my name again, telling me to look at him. I didn't budge. Then he said it was time—I had to go with him.

I was shaking like a leaf in a windstorm and hanging on to the steering wheel for all I was worth. To say I was terrified would be a huge understatement. Then I heard him speak in gentler terms as he told me the fear would go away if I would just look at him. I refused to move. I couldn't move.

What happened next was hard for me to accept, and my conscious mind wrestled with the memory. As my head was up against the steering wheel, I felt something start to touch my arm. I opened my eyes to see a grey-tan claw-like hand grasp my wrist. It wrapped its long spindly fingers around my forearm and started to pull me from the car. I never got clear whether the door was even open. I didn't think it was, but my mind rejected that, so I was never certain of that fact.

Mr. Mitchell was gently prodding the memories out of me by asking what was happening. He never, not once, asked a leading or suggestive question. I was amazed by what I was reliving, and I really struggled with what my mind was showing me. And yet, I knew it was real. *This was real—this was what had happened on that warm spring day over twenty years ago. This was the secret my mind had kept hidden away from my conscious self.*

Now I was out of the car and facing the man who'd called my name. I'd become calm the second those fingers had wrapped around my wrist. The shaking had stopped, my breathing was returning to normal, and I didn't feel as though I was going to die from fear. I looked at this man who seemed somehow familiar to me.

He was short, about 4'8". He had a large odd-shaped head with a pointy chin, huge bug-like eyes that seemed to look into my very soul and a slight body. I remember wondering how that skinny neck could hold up that heavy-looking, large head. He had only a line where his mouth should be, and I noticed right away that it didn't move when he spoke to me, yet I heard his voice clearly. He didn't appear to have any ears—just some sort of hole or indentation. His nose was also missing. There were two crevices where it should have been. His skin was grey-tan, and they were all dressed in what appeared to be one-piece coveralls that were a blue-grey color. They were all wearing hats that fit tightly on their heads.

The obvious "leader" was dressed slightly different and had an insignia on a patch located on the left side of his chest. It was a triangle with what might have been a sword or just a straight line down the middle. A red serpent or something like that wrapped itself around the centerline, and there was writing that appeared to be hieroglyphic writing on the patch.

The two creatures standing on each side of me, gripping my wrists in a vise-like hold, were similar, but I was aware of subtle differences. Their coveralls were not as dark as the leader's and they did not have any kind of ornamentation on them. They appeared to be slightly smaller, but perhaps because they were so clearly of a lesser rank, they just seemed smaller. They said nothing. The fourth fellow was still standing over by the side of the road with his wand. The guys holding onto me held their wands in their other hands while Mr. Leader was without a wand altogether.

Again I was told it was time to go.

They proceeded to walk me toward the right-hand side of the road. As we headed in that direction, I noticed a silver spaceship sitting over in the field. It looked so out of place—like it belonged on a movie set or in an amusement park. I was fascinated by it but fearful when I realized that was where they intended to take me. I tried to resist, but there was nothing I could do.

They dragged me along and appeared to not even notice that I was not helping the process. As we approached the ditch, I again became disoriented with what was happening. I seemed to "glide" along above the ground. Those wands might have had something to do with it, but I was sure that we sailed right over the fence and landed gently on the other side. They moved me along toward the ship very quickly. I pleaded to be let go.

Mr. Leader told me that wasn't possible, and all would go better if I just cooperated. I tripped and hurt myself as I went to my knees on the uneven plowed ground. They took no notice and kept moving along. Finally I just gave up and let them drag me. We were almost to the craft.

It really was an amazing thing to see. I think I could have stared at it all day long. It was shiny, silver, and sat on three, or possibly four, legs that extended down. It wasn't very big, maybe 20 feet in diameter. A ramped door was opened down to the ground, but it was very steep and without steps.

There was someone standing by the ramp as we approached. A human. No, as we got closer I could see that it was not human, but more what I would think of as "humanoid," and it was female. She was taller than the guys. She was about my height—5'5" at the time—and had somewhat large, almond-shaped brown eyes. The next thing I noticed was her hair—it was an uneven brown color and very thin and stringy, like she'd been sick. Indeed, she looked sickly with pale skin, and she was very thin and bony. She had high cheekbones that were quite pronounced and full lips. She was wearing some sort of flowing dress of a neutral color. Once again, I had the sensation of knowing her. For some reason, she had a calming effect on me. I'm not certain of this, but I think her lips moved when she talked to me. She also knew my name, and the implication was clear—she was here to help me feel more comfortable.

We were standing outside the craft, and my two captors let go of my wrists. I was told to go inside with the lady and let her help me undress.

"You Know the Drill."

"You know the drill," Mr. Leader said.

Somehow I did. Someone helped me up the ramp—I think it was the lady.

As I stepped into the ship, I was instantly aware of two things: 1) it was very, very cold in there, and 2) the interior of the ship did not match the exterior. That is, the interior appeared to be the inside of a ship that would have to measure at least 60' in diameter. It was strange and disorienting. I looked around me as I entered and felt a certain familiarity with it.

To my right was a wall that had at least one door going into another room. In front of me and to the left was a big open room with curved exterior walls; that is, they curved around, as the ship was round, but they curved down from the roof as well. It was much higher than it appeared from outside. I would have thought that I'd have to stand stooped over, but the ceiling was several feet above my head. There were lots of windows with what appeared to be benches below them.

Over to my left was an examination table with instruments and lighting above it. Against the wall and to the left of the table and beyond it was a built-in desk with chair. On the desk was what I then took to be a small television, but what I would now say was a computer. It had a keyboard in front of it. There were shelves with books or files on them.

Behind the exam table and to the right of the desk was a hallway that appeared to extend to the back of the craft. There were monitors, screens or windows built into the walls along the hallway—I couldn't get a good look to see clearly which it was. And there were doorways going into other rooms.

The lady ushered me into the room that was to my immediate right. I was instructed to remove all my clothes and get on the table. I resisted, but not for long. She stepped toward me and started to forcibly remove my clothing, all the while speaking to me in a gentle voice, telling me it was for the best. She called me by name and said it was all good. No harm would come to me. I was very shy and didn't like the idea of being naked in front of those creatures. She seemed oblivious to my concerns. In no time, I was on the table, shivering with cold and fear.

The lead guy started the exam but immediately stopped and looked at me with seeming concern. It appeared that he had become aware of my fear. He gently told me that he'd relieve my anxiety. He then stepped to the head of the table and put his hands on each side of my head. I was immediately put into a very calm state. He stepped away and instructed the woman to take his place, and so she did.

My shaking had stopped, and I was aware of the lead guy pulling down instruments from over his head and doing an "exam" on me. The other fellows all seemed to be busy with their own tasks, but Mr. Leader spoke to me in a soothing voice and explained in very simple terms what he was doing.

Every now and then he would ask me a question about my health. They were pretty general questions. He commented that I'd always had a little weakness in my legs, but they'd pretty well taken care of that. I was not able to see too much of what was going on, given that the lady was holding my head in her hands. My view was limited to looking at the lights and strange instruments above me.

At one point, he took my fingers and used an instrument to squeeze the ends of each one. He then took another instrument and scrapped my forearm in order to take a specimen of some sort. Finally, Mr. Leader, or as I came to know him, Da, said they needed to harvest my eggs.

In spite of the woman having her hands on me, I became upset. Da asked me what was wrong, and I expressed concern about what he was about to do. He wanted to know why it bothered me so much, and I replied that I wanted to have children someday. He stopped what he was doing and explained that the taking of a few of my ovum would not interfere with my ability to someday conceive. He assured me that I would go on to have children without any problem.

Then he walked to the head of the table and once again put his hands on each side of my head. He spoke to me gently, saying it was necessary and to be calm. As before, all my fear dissipated with his touch.

I watched him step to the bottom of the table and pull down a large syringe-type instrument with a long needle on the end. The woman moved to my right and held my hands. She told me to look into her eyes, and then she leaned over me to block the view. I felt a slight pressure in my lower abdomen but no pain. I did see a pale almond-yellow substance go through the tube and out of view—presumably into a container somewhere.

Then Da stepped over to the computer and did something; I couldn't see what. Mostly, I was aware of all the other guys going back to the hallway and looking at a monitor or through a window with what was a high level of expectation. I could feel the excitement as they waited for some result to show.

Then Da said, "It is good."

There was a show of celebration—even from the little worker guys. Da turned from the screen and looked at me, his large black eyes conveying what seemed to me to be a deep love and appreciation.

The woman brought my clothes to me, and I was allowed to dress. I sat on the edge of the exam table, and Da asked if I would answer some questions for him. By this time, with the exam over, I was feeling pretty comfortable and at ease, so I told him I'd be happy to try.

I guess I was expecting difficult, abstract questions because I was surprised when he started to ask what I considered to be mostly silly, inane questions like the first one: "Was I happy?"

Then he went on to ask me what I thought of the war my country was waging in Vietnam.

"What did I think of our President? Who did I vote for?" *What?* I explained that I wasn't old enough to vote.

"Did I know we were destroying our planet?"

And then some personal questions about my life. One in particular seemed strange: "Did I have sex with the boys I dated? Did I love anyone? Was I planning to marry some day?"

Then he said that I could ask him some questions since I'd been so cooperative.

"Where are you from?" was my first question.

He went over to the monitor on the desk and pushed some buttons on the "keyboard" and brought a star map up on the screen. He told me they were from a galaxy known as Andromeda and showed me on the screen where it was in relation to our system. He also told me how to find it in the night sky.

"Look for these three stars, and we are here," he said, pointing to a spec on the map.

My next question surprised everyone. "Can I go for a ride again?" I asked.

Up to this point I'd only been vaguely aware that I was really sitting in Stanley Mitchell's office in downtown Chicago, for I'd become so caught up in the reliving of the memory. It is hard to describe, but I'd been observing myself as I replayed the whole experience—kind of like watching a home movie of a past event, except that you feel everything both emotionally and physically.

From time to time, Mr. Mitchell would prompt me and ask the same few questions over and over again: "What is happening now?" or "Can you tell me what's going on now?"

A few times he asked for clarification about something I said, but I was definitely back there in that time frame. And now this question, "Can I go for a ride *again*?" shifted my awareness to my present self more than it had been at any other time during this whole process. For just a split second I wondered at the use of the word *again*.

Da "smiled" at me. That is, his eyes conveyed a warm, joyous look as he said, "So, you remember?"

He then explained that there was not time, but perhaps next time I could be taken up. As it was, I'd been there too long and was likely to have discomfort later as an after-effect.

Someone brought a glass containing a thick almond-colored substance, and I was told to drink it all down. I did as I was told. It had the substance and texture of a malt, but the flavor was not appealing. It tasted a bit like bananas and vanilla, but there was something else in it that was unpleasant, and I choked a bit on the last few swallows.

He told me the more I drank, the better off I'd be, but I would likely get sick to my stomach later that day. I asked him why that was, and he told me it had to do with the difference in the vibration between our two worlds.

I then surprised myself—that is, the observer sitting in Mr. Mitchell's office—by asking if I could stay with them and not go back to my world. I actually pleaded with him to let me stay. I told him how I had never felt like I belonged in this world and that it was a harsh place to live. I didn't like the way humans treated one another, and I'd prefer to live in their world. I talked fast as I made my case.

"Do you know that humans kill one another? And they kill animals, just for the fun of it! They are vicious, sick creatures, and I don't belong here. It is a terrible place to be."

Why couldn't I just stay with him?

I instinctively censored this part of the memory from the investigators.

Once again, I saw the love in Da's eyes as he listened to my plea. He seemed sad as he replied that they would always be around, watching out for me, and I'd be seeing them again very soon. He explained that I had to go, and my memory, as always, would be cleared of this time we spent together. I protested that little piece of news and said there was no way I was going to forget this.

"I Will Not Forget This!"

He escorted me out of the ship and told me I'd be taken back to my car now and by the time I reached my friend's house, all memory of this encounter would be erased. I looked him in the eye and told him in no uncertain terms that I would not be forgetting this.

Da appeared to laugh at my boldness, as if I were a small defiant child. Once again, the two worker Greys took hold of my arms tightly and they, along with Da, escorted me back to my car.

When we reached the little bug, I was put in my seat and the door closed. I rolled down the window and reached out to touch Da's arm again and tell him I would not be forgetting.

He smiled brightly with his eyes and said, "Yes, you will forget. You must forget."

I pulled away from them and immediately started to feel confusion about what had just happened to me. To reassure myself, I turned back to look at them, but they were gone, so I glanced over at the ship sitting in the field. I did this several times as I drove away and continued until I turned the corner and could no longer see it.

I'd begun repeating to myself over and over again the phrase "I was in a spaceship, I was with men from outer space" many times.

Fading Memories

As I made my way to Vicky's house, I became confused about why I was saying those words, but I would regain a piece of the memory and continue my chant. It felt like the experience I'd just had had been written down on a giant chalkboard and someone was taking an eraser and swiping it across the board, erasing parts of the story. There were gaps disappearing in random places, which made it hard to hold it altogether.

I reached Vicky's house in about five or six minutes, and my memory of the episode was all but gone. When I walked into her house, the first thing I noticed was the clock above the kitchen sink showing straight up noon. I was exactly two hours late. That confused me, as I was certain I had timed it so I'd be there by 10:00.

I went into another room and found another clock. It said the same thing. By now, Vicky had come flying down the stairs and said it was a good thing the cows had gotten out otherwise they would have left me since I was so late getting there.

I was in a bit of a stupor, but I still managed to blurt out to Vicky that I'd just seen little men and been on a spaceship. I insisted that she leave with me now so we could go back to see it. I heard the words come out of my mouth and was confused by the request, and yet a very small part of my mind knew it was true.

Vicky stopped her frantic movements and stood still in the middle of the kitchen looking at me for just a few seconds before she laughed a nervous laugh and ran back upstairs to finish getting ready.

I was not able to move for some time. I searched my mind trying to piece together the odds fragments of memory that were still there. I stared at the clock, knowing something was wrong other than the obvious fact that I was missing two hours of my life.

I could almost reach it—almost remember—*oh yeah, spacemen and a silver ship sitting in the field!* I could see it. I turned and raced up the stairs to tell Vicky before the image left my thoughts.

By the time I got upstairs, I forgot what it was I wanted to say to her. Instead, I ran into her father's bedroom and looked at his clock. I ran from there into the other bedroom and found another clock. Again it pointed to noon, so I went into Vicky's bedroom and looked at her clock. They all confirmed that I had lost two hours of time, yet I was unable to comprehend that information. I could make no sense of it. My memory of the experience I'd just had with Da aboard his spacecraft was gone—wiped clean from my memory.

As it turned out, there were five of us that headed off to Madison that day. I was in the backseat with Vicky and her stepsister. When we drove up the stretch of road that was adjacent to the field where the spacecraft had been sitting, I stretched my neck in an effort to see it; yet, even as I did this, I wondered what it was I was looking for. I put my head in my hands and rubbed my forehead, trying to massage the memory to the forefront, all the while not understanding what memory it was I was trying to resurrect. It was very confusing. I began to feel very tired and my stomach was a bit upset, so I closed my eyes and tried to rest.

Mr. Mitchell was asking me if I wanted to "close the door on my memories or leave it open."

I asked for an explanation of just what that entailed, and he said that if I left the door open, I'd probably gain clarity of the event we had just brought to the surface, but if I chose to have him close the door, it would repress the memory once again, and I would not have conscious recall of it. I chose to keep the door open.

Post First Hypnosis Session

My state of mind after that hypnosis session was one of shock, anger, confusion, embarrassment, and fear. I felt like Alice who had fallen into the rabbit hole and lost her way. I had walked into Mr. Mitchell's office a person confident of my place in the world, a person who moved through life with a better-than-average sense of who I was and sure of my ability to deal with whatever life handed me. I now sat there, shaken to my core, unable to grasp the meaning of my memories. I tried desperately to find a crack, a flaw, a hidden agenda, something that would undermine the whole thing and allow me to toss it aside. Even as I wrestled with my mind trying to diminish the experience, I started to gain clarity on certain points. I wanted to run.

That which does not kill you makes you stronger.

Neitzsche

Chapter 4:
Living in the House of Mirrors

Trying to Put My Life Back Together

On the long silent drive back from Chicago, I kept thinking that my father would somehow have the answers. He would make sense of it. All I would have to do is tell him what had happened, and he'd have a logical explanation. I was certain. He'd always had the answers—always knew how life operated. He'd also been the one in the family to show an interest in UFOs, so it followed that he would be the one to explain this whole nightmare away.

It was clear my husband was not equipped to deal with something as strange and unsettling as this. He'd been in the hypnotic session with me and was in a state of shock from hearing my tale. He literally distanced himself from me afterwards, choosing to walk some steps behind me as we made our way back to the car after leaving Mr. Mitchell's office. He simply wasn't capable of offering any comfort, much less reassurance.

He refused to talk about any of it on the two-hour drive home, so I kept myself calm by repeating over and over again, "My dad will explain this. My dad will explain this."

But he didn't. I was shaken to the core when he basically refused to let me even tell him about it. I tried to convey to him that I needed to talk this through, but the message I got was very clear: *Don't talk about this nonsense.*

Over the next several months, as the experiences began to happen in "real time," I went to my father in fear, seeking answers, but he shut down and closed himself off.

It turned out that it was my sister who stepped up to the plate. She was deeply fearful of what I was telling her, but I will be forever grateful that she set her own fear aside in order to be there for me. She listened to me vent and cry and rage against life for the injustice of all that was happening. She was instrumental in helping me come to terms with my father's cold reaction.

Indeed, it felt like my dad was rejecting me, not just the experience. It was very painful as I felt abandoned at a time when I needed my parents most. I was quite angry about it for a long time. My father had always been my hero—larger than life and the smartest person I knew. I will never know for certain why he could not, would not give support to me even in the form of just letting me talk. He may have had his own fear around the subject, or perhaps it was his own feelings of helplessness—his not being able to protect me—that caused him to turn away. I knew he had an interest in the subject, so it was odd to me that he wasn't even curious about what I'd experienced. It always felt like he thought I was making up stories, and this was just a ploy to get attention. To this day, he loves to watch programs about the UFO phenomenon and has always asserted that, logically, it doesn't make sense that we would be alone in the Universe.

Well, I eventually stopped trying to figure out why he shut me out and just accepted it. That helped to dissipate my anger, but I do feel sad that I was never allowed to share this journey with him.

The following weeks and months were chaotic for me. It is hard for me to find the proper words to describe what I was feeling. It was as if someone had taken a bomb and thrown it into my life—the pieces of my prior life lay in ruins around me, and I had no idea how to put them back together again. I felt isolated by my memories and became withdrawn, but I also had an obsessive need to talk to a chosen few about it. I wanted help in unraveling this mystery and, being pragmatic by nature, I wanted to make sense of it so that I could get my life back on track and move forward normally.

There is shame associated with this phenomenon. The abduction experience is the butt of endless jokes on sitcoms and movies. It is a subject that is highly ridiculed, and those of us trying to come to terms with the experience feel embarrassment and shame. For myself, I certainly didn't feel safe going to any of my friends with this, especially after seeing how my own family responded.

Making appointments with the best psychologists in the area and going in to ask about these experiences was highly traumatizing for me, but it shows just how desperate I was to gain another explanation. The shame I felt at being labeled an alien abductee has not been easy to overcome. The world does not cut us any slack on this particular topic.

In the aftermath of the regression, as the memories of that strange event became more and more clear, I found it hard to think about anything else. Little details were becoming crystal clear, and I couldn't concentrate on my work or focus on anything else. I was extremely distracted by these memories, and I had such a need to talk about them and try to process them.

I turned to Vicky. She had been there—well, kind of— during that roadside abduction. I leaned on her a lot, but it began to feel like I was burdening her with my sense of helplessness. I could see she cared deeply, but she didn't have the answers I was seeking.

I needed someone to explain to me how this was possible. Most of all, I wanted someone to make it all go away. I kept thinking that if I could find the right person, someone knowledgeable about this stuff, that individual could explain it away and thereby give me back my life. This was the major challenge I faced during this whole period of time—that feeling of being isolated without anyone to talk to who could even begin to relate to what I was going through.

Recurring Abductions and Disconnected Memories

It got even worse when the abductions started happening even as I was trying to come to terms with my memories. No sooner had I been made aware through hypnosis that I'd been abducted by aliens—not an easy thing to incorporate into your life—than I started having those experiences in real time. For so long, I worried that I'd somehow "invited" them back into my life just by opening the door to my memories. If that were so, then I decided I wanted to close that door, but it was too late for that. I knew too much at this point. So, while I was having these unbelievable experiences of terror, I somehow had to try to continue living a normal life. I had to force myself up out of bed in the morning, be with my children and family, socialize with friends, and continue to operate my business in a rational way—all the while I was living a life that felt like a horror movie.

I am a person that needs to be rational. I am practical by nature, so not being able to talk this through with someone was the worst thing for me to try to endure. I didn't feel I could trust going to any of my friends with it other than Vicky, and I could see how it pained her to not be able to help me. I knew I was expecting too much from her, but I didn't know who else to turn to. Eventually, I just shut myself off. Going to my sister was no longer an option as she was struggling with chronic depression, and I didn't want to add to her misery. As a result, I felt totally alone in the world.

One day I got a call from a sweet older lady by the name of Marion. Don had given her my number and asked her to contact me. She became a lifeline for me. Marion had had her own siting of UFOs a time or two in her life, and she was deeply interested in the subject. Her genuine concern for me and her never-ending patience in listening to me go over and over the memories that were constantly coming to the surface, placed her in the same realm as an angel or a saint. I grew to love her like she was my mother. Every now and then I would ask Don and Marion for some clue as to why and how something like this could happen, but they were so careful with their words. They provided no answers. Later I learned that they did this in an effort to keep my memories of any abduction experiences free of "contamination," and so in the best interest of the investigation, they remained neutral. Don had also requested that I not read or study anything to do with UFOs in an effort to keep me from being unduly influenced until he completed his investigation of my encounters.

As time passed, the events of the roadside abduction were becoming clearer and many, many other memories of past encounters came to the surface of my consciousness. Suddenly, so many odd occurrences came into focus. *How could I have not known that something unusual was going on in my life/had gone on my whole life? How had I diminished so many mysterious happenings and convinced myself there was nothing strange going on?*

And yet I was obsessed with proving the memories wrong. I wanted to be found insane rather than own up to these incidents that were flooding into my conscious mind. I accepted that I'd had weird events in my life, but I didn't want alien abductions to be the answer. I was way too practical, way too pragmatic, and way too sensible to accept that. More than anything, I just wanted a normal life. To that end, I searched for discrepancies and flaws in the story that had come out while under hypnosis.

Tipperary Road Incident

During the session, I'd been asked to pinpoint the location of the abduction. I stated that I was on Hwy. 92 and the closest intersection was just a bit up the road. I didn't know the name of that road. Stanley Mitchell asked me to look over at the road sign and read the name, which I did. The fact that I was able to do that fascinates me to this day. So even though I am reliving an event that happened almost twenty years ago, and I had never looked at the road sign while the event was actually happening, I was able to do it while in an induced state of hypnosis. I'm still unclear as to how that works, but Stanley Mitchell had me do a few of those types of things—check the time, look around the spacecraft, and look closely at the insignia on the leader's coveralls.

It shows just how delicate the regression/memory recall process can be. Clearly a person could easily be led off course and away from the facts of what really occurred. When I looked at the road sign, I was able to clearly see the name— Tipperary Road. So, according to my statements while under hypnosis, I was abducted on Sunday, May 12th, at about 9:45 a.m. near the intersection of Hwy. 92 and Tipperary Road.

Several weeks after the regression, I drove over to the location where the event happened. I still live in the area I grew up in and would from time to time, find myself driving down this road. Every time I would come to that rise in the road where my car had stalled, I'd feel my body start to tense. A strange sense of anxiety would come over me, and I'd often look out into the field, as if I expected to see something there.

Now, of course, I realize it was the spacecraft I was searching for. As I approached it on this day, my uneasiness had a different flavor to it. I don't know how to explain it other than to say that the memories no longer ended bluntly but flowed through me uninterrupted. It actually was a relief. I pulled to the side of the road, close to the place where my car had stalled. I looked out at the exact spot where the ship had been. There was a small ridge in the field, and I knew instinctively that was it—right there was where the silver craft had been sitting.

I sat there for a while, trying to gauge my feelings, trying to find something in me that would rise to the surface and put it all in order. I didn't really feel fear. No, it was just confusion and frustration. I pulled the car up closer to the intersection and read the name on the sign. It didn't say Tipperary Road. I stared at the sign comprehending instantly what the significance of that little piece of information meant. It didn't say Tipperary Road!

I started to tremble as the enormity of it all soaked into my brain. So my memory under hypnosis *was* wrong! Yahoo! If that was wrong, then didn't that mean that it could all be wrong? I was elated!

I drove back home feeling better than I'd felt for a long time. Instantly put behind me were the feelings of relief at finally remembering what had occurred that day and the sense of knowingness I'd felt only minutes prior. This was better. This had the potential to put my life back into a state of normalcy. It was something to build on, a starting point to dismantling all the rest of those ridiculous memories. I was going to get my life back.

My relief was short-lived. A few days later I shared my discovery with Vicky, and she calmly replied that the name of that road had been Tipperary, but it was changed some years ago. She seemed pretty certain. And she had no idea how she had just smashed to smithereens my little sliver of hope. I had never heard of road names being changed, so I resisted what she was telling me. It didn't make sense to me that a governing body would up and change a road's name. Whatever would be the reason? I searched around my office and found an old plat book and looked up the appropriate township. My heart sank as I saw, written clearly, the words "Tipperary Road," on the markings indicating that road. I felt devastated. Defeated.

Life never returned to normal. It was like I'd been given a ticket to a carnival that was filled with strange attractions and rides. I was trapped in the carnival and try as I might, I could not find my way out into the normal day-to-day life that I knew existed outside its walls. I wandered around as if in a stupor, trying to have a normal life while living in the house of mirrors. Everything was distorted. Normal failed to exist.

My mind was being flooded with images that didn't always make sense to me. One recurring memory was of me walking along a galley of some sort with Da and three other Greys. We were looking down at a huge room filled with cots. They were all lined up with narrow pathways weaving through them, and on the cots were servicemen, most in uniforms. All were unconscious. Da explained that they were being kept in an altered state of consciousness. It was easy, he said, to pick up troops while in combat. The missing time would not be noted, and they could keep a whole regimen for an extended period of time without anyone being the wiser.

I went down to the floor below and walked between the cots. I looked down at the sleeping faces of these men, most of which were so young it hurt my heart. Almost all were dressed in what must have been jungle combat attire. They were dirty and scruffy. They appeared to be mostly American, but there were some troops from the other side. I didn't understand the reason I was being shown this, nor was I told, at least to my recollection, what the purpose was for picking up all these soldiers. My visceral reaction was that they were being given a reprieve from the horrors of war, a chance to rest their minds and bodies. Perhaps they were being given a dose of "humanity."

Equal or Victim?

My recollections were starting to fall into two categories. There were those like the one noted above where I was clearly an equal to my abductors. In some instances, it felt as if they were seeking approval of the things they were doing and guidance as to the best way to go about their "work." Many times I have wondered if these beings were indeed my antecedents as the connection would feel that strong. Indeed, I clearly had a propinquity of some sort with them, but I never understood the origin.

And then there were all those many other instances where I appeared to be a victim of their "work." Taken from my car, bed, or playground and put through physical and emotional testing. No matter how many times I'd been taken, it always started out as an inimical experience. And always, my fears were calmed upon looking into their eyes or feeling their touch.

Their treatment of me ranged from cold indifference to one of overwhelming love and respect. Over the years, I came to understand that perception is everything, but in the early stages of trying to integrate these experiences into my life, I wrestled almost constantly with this aspect of the encounters. After I had reached a point of acceptance and could no longer repudiate the phenomenon, I had a strong need to draw a conclusion as to whether these beings were good or evil. So, to that end, I was eager to gain any insight I could in an effort to learn about these creatures. Over and over again, I would play through the events I knew to be true, looking for clues as to who and what these beings were. When I was asked to continue the investigation by undergoing hypnosis again, I was happy to oblige. Any shred of knowledge I could gain would be welcomed by me. I needed to learn who my abductors were and determine why this was happening.

Second Hypnosis Session

A follow-up session with Mr. Mitchell was scheduled in order to further explore the events of the roadside abduction and gain clarity on some of the more vague points. So my husband and I made the trip back down to Chicago, and I underwent another session. This one went easier and was not near the traumatizing experience I'd had the first go round since I now knew what to expect. The first regression had lasted a couple of hours, as Mr. Mitchell used a process that was known to be the most effective in extracting the truth from the witness without leading or suggesting. I'd been taken through the experience a total of three times in that first session. As the memories came to the surface, I was allowed to just relive the experience with all its emotion. I made movements and gestures as if I were there having the experience in real time.

Don reported to me later that I shivered with cold when in the ship, and I trembled with fear upon seeing my abductors. My voice quivered with emotion and fear as I relayed what I was experiencing. He said it was heartbreaking to watch. After getting through the complete story, ending with me at Vicky's house, Mr. Mitchell lifted me out of the hypnotic state for a break before taking me back down to go through it a second time.

This time he took me into a deep state of hypnosis and had me be the observer of the event. It was like I was a witness watching the event happen, and I was able to be calm and somewhat detached. I was allowed to "pull a curtain" on any of it if it became too traumatizing. With this regression, I was better able to get details of the abduction and all that occurred. Again, at the end, I was brought back out of the hypnotic state and allowed to rest for a bit before he took me back down, in order to go through the experience for the third and final time.

On this one, I was totally immersed in what was happening to me, and I was prompted to share what I was thinking and feeling. In some ways, this retelling was harder than even the first, as I was urged to explore and express my feelings. I found my thoughts became jumbled and confused as I struggled to make sense of what was happening to me.

Mainly, I couldn't rectify that feeling of knowing my captors and wanting to stay with them. I found that very disturbing as I searched within my mind to understand what that was all about and where it was coming from. I'm quite certain I kept those details to myself, somehow knowing even in that state of consciousness that those thoughts were very private and might be considered odd by my investigators.

So compared to the first regression, this second session with Mr. Mitchell was very easy and not traumatic at all. It had been several months since I'd undergone the first unnerving regression, and I'd gotten as acclimated to the abduction experience as a person could. Minor details about the events were coming to the surface, but all in all, most of the experience had been retrieved during the first session. The drive back to Wisconsin was not nearly as painful and confusing as the first had been although it was true that it took several years before my thoughts were not dominated by these memories.

Your pain is the breaking of the shell
that encloses your understanding.

Kahlil Gibran

Chapter 5:
That's No Angel. That's an Alien!

Interview with Vicky—Summer 1987

There came a point in the investigation where Don wanted to meet with Vicky and hear directly from her just what her recollection was of that day back in 1968. So one Sunday afternoon we all got together at my home, and Vicky shared what she remembered about not just that event but other strange things that had gone on during that same period of time. Vicky clearly remembered my arriving two hours late, talking about a spaceship, and trying to get her to come back with me to see it and meet the occupants.

I had a mixed reaction to hearing her talk about it. On one hand it felt good to have the outrageous story somewhat confirmed, but on the other hand I really hated having the validation of such an event in my life. I was still wishing for a mental illness to be diagnosed as that would have been easier to deal with to my way of thinking.

As we sat and talked with Vicky about those days, I couldn't deny that I'd had quite a few other incidents that had a high level of strangeness to them. The pieces were slowly coming to the surface as if they'd been held in my memory behind a wall or a block that had kept me from seeing the whole picture. We started to compare notes on some of those odd events, and it was not easy to accept the realization of just how involved these beings had been in my life.

Farmyard Abduction—Winter 1968-1969

There was one episode in particular that I had always wondered about. Now it was coming together, and what I recalled was crystal clear to me. It had occurred in the winter of 1968–1969 after the roadside abduction in May. I asked Vicky if she recalled a night when I had stumbled back into bed hours after we'd gone to sleep—feet frozen and cut with just a t-shirt on. As I talked, the events came back to me with continuing clarity.

I remembered coming awake, getting up from the bed, and walking out of the house to a spacecraft sitting on the small hill located to the east of the house. This was a much larger ship than the one involved in my roadside abduction. Again, the sight of it was surreal. Sitting on the rise with light streaming out of the many portals circumventing the ship, it was an amazing thing to behold. I walked toward it without fear. I don't recall anyone escorting me. I seemed to be walking of my own free volition. One or two beings were standing by the open ramp. The light from that opening was bright, and I could see the figures standing in shadow, but could not clearly discern who or what they were.

And then—BAM!—I was being dropped off by them. They dropped me from several feet in the air, and I hit the ground with a thump and went down in a heap. I looked up in time to see the ship rise straight up in the air and streak away silently over the top of a large building. I cried out after them to come back, but, of course, they were gone, and I was left behind in the cold and the dark.

I looked around me and tried to discern where I was, but I couldn't see a thing. I'd been in the brightly lit interior of the spacecraft just a moment ago, and now here I was in complete darkness. I was totally disoriented, and I became fearful that I was going to freeze to death. I was sure they had made a mistake and put me down at the wrong place. I stumbled around trying to find my way. My feet immediately started to ache as the ground was frozen with patches of snow and ice.

I reached out my arms and felt metal tubular fencing that seemed to enclose me. My eyes were starting to become accustomed to the dark, and I was able to make out the silhouette of a shed. I was furious with them for just leaving me there to fend for myself. I was shaking with cold and anger as I climbed over a metal gate and landed hard on some frozen dirt and ice, cutting the bottom of my foot. I walked around what I thought was the milk house but later discovered was the hog shed. I was immensely relieved to see Vicky's house right in front of me. They had dropped me in an enclosed feedlot, located in the back corner of the farmstead!

By now, my feet were really hurting, and I was shaking uncontrollably. The safety of the house seemed to be a mile away, but in truth was about 200 feet, and I quickly hobbled across the yard into the warmth of the entryway. Like many farmhouses, there was a sink and clean-up area for when the farmer came into the house. I immediately wrapped my feet in the towel that was hanging by the sink and rubbed them briskly, trying to get them warm. Oh, how they ached.

How could they do that? It was freezing out; I could easily have died if I'd not found my way out from behind that shed.

I was starting to feel confused. Up to this point it seems my anger at them had kept the memory of what I'd just experienced alive and in the forefront of my thoughts, but now it was falling away fast.

What had I been doing outside at this time of the night— with barely any clothes on? Had I walked in my sleep?

I'd never known myself to do that.

What had I been doing out behind the shed?

I clearly remembered being there and climbing over the gate.

As I ran the water waiting for it to get warm, I leaned across the sink and looked closely at myself in the mirror. I looked deep into my eyes and tried so very hard to see who I really was. I knew the image that I was seeing was not me. There were secrets there behind those brown eyes, and I'd known those secrets only moments before. I tried to grab hold of them, but it was like trying to catch a butterfly. I would reach out to touch it, but I could never quite grasp it. At best, I would feel the soft brush of the wings against my hand, so I knew it was real—it was there—but I could never quite close my fingers around it.

I soaked a portion of the towel in the warm water and cleaned my feet as best I could. They were frozen and the warmth of the towel caused them to ache even more. I cried as I rubbed them, but it wasn't just because of the pain. It was the confusion I was experiencing. A feeling of abandonment had come over me and an overwhelming visceral sadness. I was homesick. I wanted to go home—not home to my parents' house but *home.*

The Babysitting Abduction

Vicky also remembered an incident that happened during this same period of time in 1968. We were at the farm but not in the main house. Her older sister, husband, and young son lived in a small second house on the farm. It was a weekend night, and we were babysitting her nephew. I do remember most of this, but Vicky helped to fill in the blanks. The house was very small, and the baby was in bed sleeping. We were sitting out in the little living room watching TV and drinking sodas.

I remember starting to feel very anxious and nervous.

"They're coming for me," I told Vicky.

"Who? Who is coming for you?" she asked.

I didn't know. I just looked at her, trying to figure out an answer.

"You need to protect me. Don't let them take me!" I heard myself say.

She didn't know how to respond.

I jumped up and said, "Hide me in the basement."

I ran to the basement door and pulled it open. I looked down into the dark, dank space and knew that was not going to work. I slammed the door shut and headed for the bedroom. I was frantic. I knew they were out there and coming for me.

"Hurry!"

We scrambled into the bedroom and jumped into her sister's bed and covered ourselves with the bedspread. The bed was up against an outside wall and that was the side I was on. I pushed my back up tight against the wall and had Vicky in front of me on the other side as a barrier. I peered out at the doorway, watching for them.

There was a loud buzzing sound and the feeling of electricity in the air. Now they were very close.

Oh no! How could I be so stupid! They would just reach in through the wall and take me.

And with that thought, I lost all memory except for a very faint vision of a saucer sitting up on the rise where it always landed when it came to the farm for me. But here's the intriguing part: Vicky remembers all this exactly the same, including the loud buzzing sound—which she accurately describes as more of a vibration—but she fell asleep and woke up some time later, and I was gone from the bed.

The next thing we both knew, her sister and husband were standing in the doorway, scolding us for crawling into their bed. We told them that a UFO had been there earlier and that we'd tried to hide from it, but they just laughed at us. We trudged sleepily up to the main house and into Vicky's bedroom.

Neither of us really ever forgot about this incident, but it's like all the other strange memories: you just bury them. You don't think about it. When you have no parameters to put the event into and no reality to connect it to, the tendency is to just abandon the whole thing. Forget about it as best you can and not look too closely at it because there are no answers to be found. Add to that the blocking methods used by the ETs and before you know it, the event is such a hazy memory that may just as well be a dream.

The Bee Incident

It was right around this same time that Vicky and I shared another very odd event. It was a hot summer day, and being typical teenagers, we spent it lying in the sun. But by about 2:00 we got tired of it, and the sun was past its peak anyway, so we decided to go for a walk down the road. I don't think we'd ever done that before, so we must have been pretty bored to even think of it, but we set off with the goal of making it down to the nearest intersection, which would have been a little less than a mile away. As we walked along the quiet country road, our talk was mostly about the boys we had crushes on and who we were dating or hoped to date—typical talk for 17-year-old girls. I don't think we encountered one single car or truck on our afternoon jaunt, so we moseyed along, walking right down the center of the road.

We were about halfway to our turn-around point when a bee suddenly started to dive-bomb me. I don't have a fear of bees even though I've been stung a time or two, but I realize it has to land on you first to do any damage, so I usually don't panic but just dodge it or swat it away. I also don't believe in killing them unnecessarily, but this bee was on a suicide mission. He dived at my face, tried landing on my nose, buzzed my eyes, and even got tangled in my hair. It was ridiculous. He was like a crazy kamikaze pilot. I tried everything but eventually ended up running down the road in an effort to get away from him. I've never in my life encountered anything like it, which is why I remember this day so well. It was, well, just so ridiculous. Vicky and I later referred to it as "The Day the Bee Chased Us down the Road."

The reason I mention this incident is because of the way the walk ended. Things got kinda strange. I was a good distance ahead of Vicky as I'd been trying to get away from the bee, so I was almost to the end of this road and the intersection where we intended to turn around when I decided that I needed to go down a little side road that was someone's driveway and check out their house. A strange high pitched tone that was more of a vibration had started ringing in my ears, and it made me feel very anxious.

I remember Vicky yelling after me, asking me what I was doing, and I said something really odd. I said these people were on vacation, and I needed to make sure the place was safe. Even as I said it and heard those words, I knew I was talking nonsense. I didn't have any idea who might live there, and I certainly could not know if they were on vacation, but I walked down that little driveway and turned at the bottom of the incline and went out of sight of Vicky.

Suddenly, I found myself standing amongst some bushes and looking at the trees and wondering what I was doing. It felt as though I had just come awake. I was confused and perplexed as I tried to understand what was going on. It felt as if I was coming up from some deep, dark place as I slowly recalled the walk Vicky and I were on. My head was ringing as I bolted from the tangle of bushes I was caught in and ran back up to the main road. Vicky was still standing where I'd left her, and as I sprinted up to her, she fell in step with me, and we continued to jog back toward her home.

After a bit, we stopped and the two of us walked slowly toward the farm, but something was "off." We were both very subdued, and the lively chatter we'd enjoyed on the walk down the road was forgotten. I felt overwhelmingly tired and was still feeling the anxious, unsettling sensation, but it was more than that. Something wasn't right. The bright sunny day had faded to long shadows, and I checked my watch but felt it had to be broken because it was a good two hours later than it should be.

I was just starting to ask Vicky about it when we heard her dad turn on the milking machines in the barn.

Oh my god, he was starting to milk?

Again, I looked at my watch and reported to Vicky that somehow it was now close to 5:00. We looked at each other in a panic. I searched for the sun and found it behind me—low enough on the horizon to validate the time. It didn't make sense, but we didn't have opportunity to analyze it. We were expected to help her dad with chores, so we ran at a dead heat toward the house in order to get changed and out to the barn.

I don't believe we ever talked about the missing time to any great extent. We did discuss the suicidal bee, but after a few feeble attempts to try to figure out where the time had gone, we simply let it go. There was no rational answer, so there was no sense in discussing it.

I eventually came to understand that the visits from my guys, the Greys, usually consisted of a number of encounters over a period of time, and then they would disappear from my life for long stretches. The roadside incident occurred when I was seventeen years old, and it was evident from both my newly acquired memories and Vicky's recollections that I'd had a good number of visits from them over a 12-18-month span. As best I could figure, they would be around from two months to more than a year and then leave for months or even years.

Around the time of my pregnancies, they were clearly more involved. Their visits would be sporadic and random with abductions occurring 2-4 times a week and then nothing for several days. Their visits occurred during the day just as much as at night. The time I spent with them was anywhere from 1-3 hours, but there were times when I was missing well over eight hours at a stretch. These were all physical experiences, not the astral visits that would later become more the norm.

Brief Peace—Marriage, Multiple Moves 1970

It appears that the high level of activity I had during the year of 1968 came to an end sometime that following spring or summer, and I had relative peace in my life until 1970 when I decided to marry at only nineteen years of age. I'd only been married a short time when it felt crucial that we have our first child. That had not been our plan since my husband was a full-time student and financially it was just not feasible. But, nonetheless, I pushed and pushed and argued my case until finally Tom relented.

Clearly, I had been programmed by the Greys to start our family at this time against all rationale. Looking back, it's easy to see that Da and his gang were back in my life at this time as I have the same types of partial memories, strange memories of encounters and missing time events that point to their presence. It appears that they were around for a good long time during these early years of my marriage and motherhood.

Thanksgiving Incident—1971

It was Thanksgiving of 1971. I was twenty years old and still a newlywed. My husband and I were living in a cheap two-bedroom apartment in a small community outside Madison. We had only recently moved into this apartment and weren't even unpacked yet. We'd been moving every couple of weeks, and if you'd asked me why we were doing that, I would not have had an exact answer, but I'd always find an excuse.

We'd been married for less than a year and had moved five times already. This pattern continued throughout the first four years of our marriage. Indeed, we moved no less than nineteen times in those four years. My husband got fed up with it and all the teasing we took from our relatives.

Once I even packed us up and moved without telling him. It was during his final exams, and since I barely saw him during that time, I never got a chance to tell him. I just left a note for him on the door, telling him where I'd moved us to, along with a map so he could find me.

I know that's hard to believe, but it's true. I was trying to hide, of course, but even *I* didn't understand it back then. It quickly got to the point where no friends or relatives would help us anymore, but it didn't matter. We owned very little, and we could do the job ourselves in a day or two.

I had gotten home from work and was trying to find something to fix for our dinner. We were very poor and at times our cupboards would get quite empty. This was one of those times.

My husband was at school taking exams but was due home later that evening. I was standing in the kitchen when I heard a noise from the back bedroom. I stepped from the cupboard and walked out into the middle of the room to look back toward the place where the noise had originated when there was a huge flash of light from the second unused bedroom and at the same time a deafening crack like a giant bat had hit a baseball.

I remember movement in the spare bedroom and the sound of scurrying feet—the apartment had hardwood floors, and it sounded like a couple of squirrels were running around.

My heart started to pound, and I turned to run out the door when I glanced back over my shoulder toward the bedroom. What I saw was completely rejected by my mind. All I have is a faint recollection of a couple of little creatures coming out of the second bedroom. They were moving very quickly toward me with fast, jerky movements that didn't seem to be happening in real time. That is, it was like a time-lapsed movement. It happened so fast I couldn't focus on what they looked like as they grabbed ahold of me.

Then all time was lost until later when I came stumbling out of the second bedroom. I remember wondering what I was doing in there.

Had I been looking for something in one of the boxes? Yes, that must be it. I must have been looking for something.

But I felt strange, and as I now see was a pattern, I went into the bathroom and stared at myself in the mirror as if I could find the answer to my confusion if I just looked into my own eyes long enough. I was quite disoriented when my husband returned from school, exhausted from exams and work.

I began to pester him and insist that we make love. He tried to beg off due to his being thoroughly fatigued, but I was unrelenting. I heard myself say that this was the optimum time for me to conceive and that it was imperative that we do it NOW!

I clearly remember wondering why I thought that.

How would I even know such a fact? Lastly, why was I being so damn inconsiderate of my husband's feelings? As I made my argument, it felt as if the words were not my own but had been programmed into my mind. Now I have no doubt whatsoever about that point.

Our oldest daughter was conceived that evening. Always, when I would reflect back on that bizarre night, I would remember the odd feeling that someone was watching us. I complained to my husband that I was sure someone was peeking in and spying on us. He got up and checked the windows, but I knew that wasn't where they were—they were in the closet. So I got up and opened the closet door to search for someone—my sense was that strong.

Many times I have reflected on the strange events of that night, but that overwhelming feeling of being watched was so strong that it was the *one* thing that stood out most—more than the brilliant flash of light or the larger-than-life sound that defied logic and more than the creepy sound of the scurrying feet.

I packed up and moved us out of that apartment within days of this event occurring. I had become very, very fearful of being there and found I had anxiety whenever I had to enter the building. My memory of that night was blurry, and I never even told anyone about it. It was kept pretty well blocked for a good long while, but because of my anxiety about the place, I kept trying to figure out what had happened.

I knew there was a memory, but I just couldn't seem to get to it. One thing was for certain—whatever it was, it scared the hell out of me. So we moved out before we even got unpacked. We'd lived there for less than three weeks.

The Stone House Abduction—February 1972

This time it was a cold, damp farmhouse that we moved into, and once again I made a vow to myself to stay put for a while and make this place into a home. Tom wasn't the only one tired of moving. I was exasperated with myself and tired of the jokes.

We'd been living in this stone house for less than three months when I had an encounter that I was able to keep in my awareness—well, at least the parts leading up to the abduction and immediately after. It was February of 1972. My husband was still a full-time student at the university, and he also drove a truck part-time to help support us. I was about two months pregnant with our first child and working as an aide in the recovery room at a local hospital.

It was early morning, and Tom had left before dawn for work and school. My shift started at 7:30 a.m., so I had to leave the house by 6:45 in order to make it on time. I'd awakened to a cramping sensation in my lower abdomen, and I was spotting blood, so I put a call into my doctor. While I waited for a return call, I also called in to work to tell them I would not be in that day. I hastily hung up the phone in order to not miss the call back from the doctor. I was alone at the house, and I tried my best to stay calm.

Soon enough the phone rang, and I spoke with my gynecologist. He told me to stay in bed for the day and come in if it got worse. He assured me this was not unusual, and that while I could be miscarrying, it was most likely not the case. In any event, there was nothing to be done at this juncture except rest.

I sat at the kitchen table, concentrating hard on every word he said, my heart pounding as I struggled not to cry. The house was cold, and I sat huddled in a blanket with the phone cord stretching from the phone across the room to where I sat facing the wall. After the doctor hung up, I stayed hunched over in my chair, my back to the room, cradling the phone in my hands. I was silently crying and saying a prayer, asking that my baby be protected and allowed to continue its growth within me when I suddenly became aware of a shuffling sound coming from the back entryway.

It moved very, very quickly and came to a stop behind me; someone was standing in back of me. I made a movement to turn around, but hands came down on my shoulders and stopped me. My name was spoken softly, and I was told not to turn around.

Then as always, the words, "It is time."

The next thing I knew I was coming awake, but I was no longer in the kitchen. I was lying curled up on a bed somewhere. I pushed myself up with both arms and looked around. My head was foggy, and I was disoriented. I couldn't place where I was, but I noticed the light in the room was growing dim. There was a window to my right, and I stared out at the darkening sky, trying to make sense of it. I knew it was no longer morning—that much was clear from the look of the sky.

Slowly, it was starting to dawn on me that I was in our bedroom, but I was disoriented because I was upside down in the bed. My head was in the lower right hand corner, and my feet were up toward the top. My thoughts were heavy, and I felt as if I was coming out of a drug-induced state.

Then I saw my husband lying on the floor near the doorway that led into the bedroom. It startled me as he looked as though he'd been walking to come into the room and had simply tipped over. He was not in a natural pose, but before I could contemplate it any further, something caught my attention in the mirror that hung above the dresser.

There was a woman reflected in the mirror. I looked for some time to make sure I was really seeing the image, and then I turned to look at her directly. It was the same lady from the roadside abduction, but, of course, I didn't know that then as that memory was still buried and would be for another seventeen years. She was wearing a light-colored garment that went down below her knees, but her feet were not visible. She simply faded away right above her ankles.

Years later, I would tell my daughter the story of how an angel that looked like a sickly Native American woman came to me in the early stage of my pregnancy and proclaimed that all was well.

Her exact words were, "Do not worry. You will not lose the baby. It is important she be born."

And then she faded away. I never forgot that incident. I truly did think of it as an angelic vision even though the angel was not exactly what I would have conjured up in my mind as an example of the ideal messenger of God.

I loved sharing the story with my daughter as I thought it was a wonderful example of how we are being watched over by our Heavenly Father. Of course, all that changed when I underwent the hypnosis session in Chicago and made the connection. That was no angel—that was an alien.

Eventually, I told Don about this incident. We were trying to decide which of my abduction memories we should explore next, and this one seemed like a good choice. I had conscious memories leading up to the event as well as after. I definitely had missing time—I'd lost more than eight hours! And there were witnesses who had heard me tell the story about that day and my encounter with the Native American angel.

After the incident at the stone farmhouse, we moved again. As before, I could no longer tolerate being in that house. My anxiety and fear kicked in each and every time I had to enter it, and I could not stand to be there alone. This time we went into a motel room. I had exhausted all our options of apartments in the area, and this was the best thing we could come up with on short notice.

Motel Incident

I have always remembered a particular night when I was feeling pretty content as I actually liked living in a single room—it felt safe. Best of all, I had a tub that I could take a bath in! It was early evening as I filled the tub with water and carefully lowered myself down into its warmth. I was always struggling with being cold and rarely felt comfortable even in the summer. I let the warm water cover me like a blanket. I lay like that for some moments before my eyes rested on my tummy. I was just starting to show, and my hands were rubbing my small bulge protectively as I thought how wonderful it was to have a life growing inside of me. Then I noticed some red marks. I looked closer and saw that there were eight needle marks in a circle on my stomach. I stared in disbelief. I could hear the blood pounding in my ears as I sat motionless trying to comprehend. Even though I was sitting in warm water, I went cold with fear. And then I became hysterical.

My cries echoed off the small bathroom walls. I cursed them. I railed against them all the while not knowing *who* it was I was venting my anger at, but somehow, somewhere, in the deep recesses of my mind, I knew. I knew. I struggled with the idea of calling my doctor the next morning. I knew I should, but I wasn't sure this was anything he'd be able to explain, and I was so terribly frightened.

Hiding from Reality

Looking back, I see clearly that I tried to hide from the reality of the marks I'd seen there on my tummy as the implications were too disturbing for me to face. I simply couldn't deal with it. The idea that harm could come to my baby was more than I was willing to accept. So while I went back and forth about what to do, the issue resolved itself—the circle of red needle marks were gone late morning of the following day.

I did my best to convince myself that I hadn't really seen anything at all—that it had all just been my imagination. I really needed it to not be true, but I could never lie to myself that well—and I never could bring myself to tell anyone about it. My fear was that if I spoke the words aloud, it would make it real. Better to never speak of it. I hung onto the words of my "Indian angel" for all I was worth and prayed that her assurances were for real. And in the meantime, I cursed the demons that would do such a thing to my baby.

I never did make the connection between the needle marks and what had happened previously at the stone farmhouse. All those years, and I never once connected the two events or questioned it. That is, until I underwent hypnosis and recognized the lady present during that roadside abduction as being the very same woman who'd been standing in the corner of my bedroom.

Now I've come to understand that she is almost always present during my abduction experiences. That's how very strange this whole phenomenon is. I have always had a hard time with the way they were able to block my level of awareness. That is, it would be "normal" for a person to look at some of these experiences—whether it's missing time or partial memories—and be obsessed with trying to connect the dots or make sense of it. But that doesn't happen with the abduction experience. You don't see the high level of strangeness, or if you do, it is short-lived. It fades from your thoughts more quickly than a chance encounter with an acquaintance at the grocery store.

When Don and I discussed what abduction memory we wanted to explore next, it was an easy choice for me because I wanted to understand exactly what had happened. There were many anomalies that occurred during my pregnancy, and I wanted answers.

My beautiful, sweet daughter was born about three weeks early when I became toxic, and labor was induced. It turned into an emergency C-section when things got dicey, but all was perfect in the end.

She was seventeen years old when I made the trip to Chicago to undergo hypnosis in an effort to understand what role, if any, the Greys had played in the formation of her life. She was unaware of these events as I had never shared any of the stories with her other than the "Indian Angel" story. I was trying to keep my daughters protected from the surreal events going on in their mother's life, but it turned out that was not an easy thing to do.

When you get to the end of your rope,
tie a knot and hang on.

Franklin D. Roosevelt

Chapter 6:
Blue Lights & Bruises

Increasing Incidents

The continuing clarity of my abduction experiences along with the eventual recognition that something surreal was going on even as I struggled to come to terms with the memories was almost more than I could bear. It was taking a huge toll on my marriage, my relationship with my family, my daughters, and my work. I felt totally alone and extremely vulnerable. I was near my breaking point, but knew I had to stay strong for my daughter's sake. Little did I know that the journey was just beginning, and the limits to which I would be pushed were not even on the horizon.

The Night of the Blue Light—June 1988

It was a warm Friday night in June of 1988 when an incident occurred that we eventually came to refer to as "The Night of the Blue Light." My daughters both had someone spending the night with them at the house. I had been encouraging them to stay with friends or have friends stay over as much as possible so as to add another layer of protection for them. Tom usually worked late on Friday nights, but he'd left work early to come home. I had started to get that anxious "they're coming" feeling earlier in the evening, and I had called to ask him to please come home as soon as possible.

It was about 2:30 in the morning when I awoke to the smell of sulfur, like someone had lit a match. I was in a very deep sleep, and I had a hard time pulling myself up out of it. I sat up in bed and sniffed the air. It seemed to fade, so I lay back down. Again, it was very strong, so I sat back up—this was difficult because I literally felt drugged. I did this three times before finally convincing myself that I needed to wake up as the house could be on fire! Tom was sleeping soundly. I heard our dog start to howl out on the lawn. It was a half bark, half whine sound that I'd never heard from him before, and it was very unnerving.

I remember thinking, *Poor thing. It's like he knows he should bark to protect us, but clearly he is scared to death of something.*

Next, I heard scurrying sounds from downstairs, so I jumped out of bed and went to investigate. As I walked across my bedroom and onto the balcony that overlooked the living room, I became aware of a blue light shining in through the skylights and west bedroom window. It was eerie. It seemed to be pulsing. I went downstairs and heard noise from my youngest daughter's bedroom.

Both my daughters and their friends were out of bed and peering through the window blinds. They were all talking at once, and it was clear they were frightened. They told me that someone had been shining a blue light in the window and that he'd been calling out to them.

They'd heard him say in a sing-song voice, "Hello...hello."

I had them turn off all the lights in the house, and I left them to go outside and investigate. I was certain one of my daughter's friends was out there pulling a trick, a very cruel trick. As I went out the front door, an electrical charge went through me and enveloped the house. The doorbell made a funny buzzing sound and seemed to burn out. All four girls came running out of the bedroom as I turned and jumped back into the foyer. I started up the stairs to get Tom just as he came out of the bedroom and raced down the steps. We told him what had happened, and he quickly bolted out the front door and searched around the house, looking to see who might be there.

Finding nothing, he took our car and drove down the road, back and forth, trying to find out if some pranksters had left their car parked down the street or if there were kids running away from our house. Again, he found nothing. And that was the end of it, except our dog disappeared for a few days. Poor thing must have been terrified and decided to run.

A few years later, when I asked my oldest daughter what her recollection of that night was, she told me that when they heard someone calling to them, they figured it was a friend, but when they looked out on the lawn they saw a short man with oddly long arms standing, as if at attention, and he was calling her name.

She also recalled that I had come out onto the upstairs balcony and with a strange look on my face, had announced, "They're here" before turning around and going back into my bedroom.

There were other discrepancies, as well—something I've since learned is typical of these encounters as the highly emotional state you are in colors your perception. Plus, the Greys use screens and blocking techniques to keep you protected.

The morning after the "blue light" incident, my youngest daughter and her cousin came running in from outside and asked me to come look at something with them. Out beyond our manicured lawn where the grass was left to grow long was a circular area where the grass had been flattened in a swirling pattern. It was only about twelve feet in diameter, but I knew instantly what it was. This was west of the house—the direction from which the blue light had come the night before. It was more physical evidence that what was happening was not just being created in my mind. These were real *honest to goodness* physical experiences—as if I needed more proof.

My daughter and her cousin wanted to know if this is where a UFO had landed. I said, "No, looks to me like some rain fell here and created a natural swirling area."

My daughter said, "I think it's where they landed. Like before. Remember when you showed Amy and me where they land—it looked just like this."

Discovery of Daughters' Drawing

All my motherly instincts came to the surface, and I repeated my earlier explanation, but she would have nothing to do with it. I looked deep into her brown eyes as she explained fervently how I'd brought her and her sister out to this same spot a few years ago and shown them the place a UFO had landed. She continued to say that I'd actually sat them down at the kitchen table and had them draw a picture of what they thought a flying saucer might look like, as well as the occupants!

I was dumbfounded.

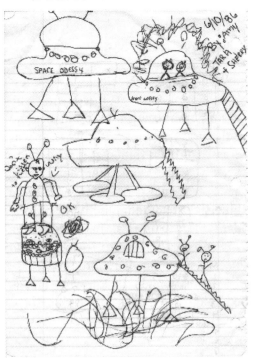

Why was my child saying these things? Her cousin was listening to this all with wide eyes, but said nothing. I was baffled.

Then my sweet daughter said, "You didn't want us to be scared when we saw them, remember?"

I most certainly did not remember. And that did not sound like something I would do, not if I were in my right mind.

"You put the drawing in your hope

chest, so you'd have it for proof."

Good grief! This just kept getting more and more strange.

"Ahhh, well, let's just go take a look," I said.

And we all three marched into the house to go look for the evidence that I knew would not be there. Except it was. It was a piece of lined notebook paper that I'd dated and saved. On it was the childish drawing of an alien and spaceships.

My daughter was talking again, saying, "Remember, you said not to be afraid if we see them. You said they wouldn't hurt us, but they might look scary because they don't look like us."

My daughter was almost thirteen years old now. So that meant she would have been about eleven years old, and her older sister nearly fourteen when I had them do the drawing, as it was dated June of 1986—a full year before the whole thing had started. I couldn't believe it.

If I hadn't seen that sheet of paper for myself, I would never have believed I would do such a thing. To my own daughters! I now understand that once again I'd been programmed to do this, but it is frightening to think these things were happening without my consent or approval. It was one thing when it involved just me, but these were my children. Two innocent children. I was sick.

I suppose an argument could be made that it was done in an effort to lessen the trauma should they be witness to my encounters, but it still angered me to no end. Fear for my children welled up in me, and the anger I felt toward these intruders was escalating once again.

It left me wondering, *What else had happened in my life that I had no recollection of? How many missing pieces were there? Does everyone have this kind of thing going on, but I had somehow managed to open the door to it?*

And then again, the final thought—*I must be completely insane.*

After this latest episode, the final broken pieces of my life seemed to turn to dust in my hands. The overwhelming evidence was that this was really happening and had been going on my entire life. It was a hard fact to accept. The idea was constantly being played through my thoughts as I went from trying to pretend that nothing was going on to examining every shred of evidence to try to understand what it was all about. It was exhausting. I'd been trying very hard to hang onto some form of normalcy in my life, but now it felt as if I'd slipped over into another dimension entirely. This is from the diary I kept during this time:

I continue to be baffled by all that has happened and continues to happen. I want concrete answers, but realize I will probably never get them. And sometimes that sends me into a panic. I don't understand. Is this real? I just don't know what to make of all this. I know, or at least I think I know, that certain things are real—physically real. But don't crazy people believe in their reality? I'm so confused, and I get angry cause I just want to understand.

A Benefit of Experiencing These Encounters

I was, however, able to find an upside to these encounters—well, eventually, I found a few, but one of the more positive aspects I became aware of early on was the added bonus that comes from being subjected to the higher vibrations for prolonged periods of time. I was mother to a spirited teenager, and it came in handy at times to be able to utilize some of the gifts afforded me by that exposure.

More than once I was able to direct my thoughts to my daughter in order to "check in on her" and make sure all was well. There was one night when I had a sense she was not where she had told me she was going to be. I felt quite certain she was with a boy that I really didn't approve of at that time. There had been an incident where he'd dropped her off on the front porch in a condition that no mother wants to find her daughter, so I'd restricted her from spending time with this young fellow.

That evening it was a very simple thing for me to "push" my awareness out in search of my daughter. I was feeling a deep sense of foreboding, and I just needed to know she was safe. I sat in my bedroom on the edge of my bed as I directed myself out of my body and moved rapidly across the valley toward the location of my daughter. It was as simple as thinking the thought. It happened quite easily and spontaneously.

Within no time at all, my awareness was hovering above some trees and looking at what appeared to be a tri-level house with a couple of cars parked outside it. I remember the family dog barking at me. I found it interesting that he was able to sense or see my energy there as I moved closer to the house. It felt as if I were peeking in a window, only I wasn't.

I was there in the room, looking down at my daughter who was stretched out on the floor in front of the TV. Another couple was on the sofa. I took note of the pattern in the carpet and the color of the sofa; for some reason that struck me and stayed with me. I heard the young man, the same young man I'd forbidden my daughter from seeing, call out to her from the other room. Then he came walking into the room and handed her a plate with a grilled cheese sandwich on it. Everything looked harmless enough, so I left but returned in body to retrieve my daughter.

Later when she asked how I knew she was there, I told her of my experience and was very convincing as I described in detail the room and the words I'd heard spoken. After that, my daughter tended to obey my orders a little more carefully. So not everything associated with the Greys could be categorized as painful or frightening. There were definitely some positive aspects.

Not a Dream Incident

A week or two after the night of the blue light incident, I had a very strange experience. I had a dream that I was having a dream. Only I knew it wasn't a dream. I'd come "awake" during an abduction. Five of the little worker guys were carrying me through the tall grass out behind our house. I was pleading with them over and over again to put me down. Their hands were all over me, and I hated it. The night was cool and damp. The grass was wet against my backside, and I was chilled.

Then it seemed as if I were waking from a dream, and I remember thinking, *Oh good, it was just a dream.*

But they were still there, only now we were in the bedroom and they were putting me back into my bed. Again, their hands all over me, handling me. It was such a helpless feeling. I hated it. Such an intrusion, so demeaning and invasive. I was unable to do anything; I was helpless.

Again, I came awake from my dream. This time they were gone, and I was, of course, in my bed. I considered that memory and pondered it quite a bit. Clearly, they put you into an altered state of consciousness much like sleep, but in this case I actually was able to come up out of it a few times. And it felt like coming awake from a dream, only it was most certainly *not* a dream. This was real. I knew it at the time, and I had total recall of it the next morning. It was a very disturbing experience.

Black Helicopter Visits

Most of my abduction experiences took place during the daytime, at least those encounters were the ones I had the clearest memory of, but I certainly had my share of nighttime encounters. If all I'd had over the course of my life were night abductions, it would have been far easier for me to dismiss all this as nothing more than dreams, night paralysis, or hallucinations of some sort, but because so many of my encounters occurred during the day—and I had such clear memories and in some cases witnesses—it was not so easily dismissed. This nighttime experience was rare, but I couldn't dismiss it as a dream. Not in view of all that had been occurring in my life during this period of time. All the other components were there to indicate it was a real, physical experience.

It was also soon after the "Night of the Blue Light" incident that I started to notice the black helicopters around my house. This happened incessantly. For weeks and weeks they would buzz over my house, sometimes hovering right over my roof. Usually it was just one, but on some occasions there would be as many as three. I often wondered what my neighbors thought about it as there was no way you couldn't notice. It tapered off after a few months but didn't end completely until the encounters with the ETs stopped. I talked to Don about it and later learned it was probably our military keeping tabs on me and my visitors.

Ready for Third Hypnosis Session—Fall 1988

As a means of coping and trying to gain understanding of what was happening to me, I was ready to undergo a third hypnosis session with Mr. Mitchell. We made another trip to Chicago in the late fall of 1988. It had already been decided that the "Indian Angel" episode would be the one we would focus on since I had a fair amount of conscious recall of the events leading up to it as well as the aftermath. Everyone who was close to me had heard the story, as well as my bewilderment as to what had really happened that day. I was fearful about what I might learn from this regression since this involved not just me but my precious baby. Even though I knew all was well with her, it was still upsetting to think aliens had somehow played a part in her conception and might have been present during the term of my pregnancy.

By this time, my husband had withdrawn a fair amount from our marriage. I know he was questioning my sanity and was feeling fearful of the things that had started to happen at our home. I do believe he tried to the best of his ability to be there for me; it's just that he had nothing to draw on. He was in a position to pull back, and I suppose I really couldn't blame him for it. Certainly, I would have hidden from it if I could have!

Tom had experienced his own encounter with a flying saucer one night when he was driving semi in the early years of our marriage. It had a big impact on him and had left him rattled. He didn't like to talk about it. And, of course, there was the episode that he shared with our youngest daughter of seeing the flying disc over our house the same night I'd seen the big white globe with orange lights during the UFO flap. Still I think in his mind, he found a way to rationalize it—minimize it—and somehow make it all okay by convincing himself that is was me who was crazy.

Restaurant Incident with Tom

There was a day when we went to lunch together, and I was having a terrible time. I really didn't feel as if I could go on anymore. The intrusion into our home by these beings was not something I felt equipped to deal with. It was all so confusing to me and out of control. Nothing made sense anymore, and the sheer terror of it was wearing on me. I had been trying so hard to find a way to dismiss all this UFO stuff, but with the things going on at our house, it was becoming increasingly hard for me to mark it up to displaced memories or mistaken recall while under hypnosis.

The marks were right there on my body and all the mounting evidence was hard to ignore. I felt as though I'd been beaten into submission—somehow forced to believe the unbelievable. Over lunch, I started to vent and express my fears and concerns to my husband, but he looked at me with vacant eyes, and I knew he didn't want to hear any more of this craziness.

I became angry. I needed someone to understand the strain and stress I was feeling. My God, my recollection was that I'd been with aliens the night before. What is a person supposed to do with that kind of information? Was I really expected to just sit there and talk about the weather?

Suddenly, I stopped talking. I looked at him intently for a moment and then softly said, "Roll up your sleeves."

The fear registered immediately in his eyes. Somehow he knew where I was going with this. He sat stone still. Again, I hissed at him, "Roll up your sleeves!" This time he did. I reached over and turned his wrists up, and there on his forearm were finger bruises. The marks left by the aliens when they drag you by the arms while you are either unconscious or are struggling against them. It was one thing to see them on me but another thing entirely to see them on his own body.

That was what I wanted. I wanted someone else to know it was real. Not a story. Not imagination. I could see my husband was shaken to his core, but he slowly and deliberately rolled up his sleeves, stood up, and calmly walked out of the restaurant. We never talked about it. He just withdrew even more.

I don't really understand how I knew those finger bruises would be there on his forearm. Again, that is part of the high level of strangeness that surrounds this subject. Did I know because in the deep, dark corners of my mind I had a memory of him being dragged out of our bed by them? Did the bruises appear because "they" put them there in an effort to support me? Did I somehow manifest them? I might never know, but as time goes by, it appears that my questions do get answered, so I guess it is reasonable to assume that this one will also be explained eventually.

We decided to go into Chicago the night before the regression. It was cold and snowy as we searched for a hotel room that was within driving distance of the CUFOS office. We thought it would be good for us to get away and have a little time to ourselves. We had left our daughters staying with friends and were determined to make the best of this little getaway. But the strain and stress of the past several months had taken a toll on us, and we felt like strangers. We checked into the room, had a light dinner and turned in early.

Men in Black (MIB) Episode

Had I known what was in store for me, I would never have gone within a hundred miles of that hotel room. My memories of that night are deeply buried, and that is where I'd like to keep them. I have faint flashes of three hulking men coming to the room. They are big and burly, dressed in old-fashioned dark suits with vests and wearing hats and wide leg pants.

They beat my soul. That is the only way I know how to put it. I'd never, before this incident, heard of the phenomenon known as "The Men in Black" (MIB). It is one of the most bizarre aspects of the alien abduction scenario. How they fit into the program, I have no idea, but they certainly appeared to have had a vested interest in what was going on with me.

I'd been programmed with a message to give to Don Schmitt, and that was all that kept coming out of my mouth the following morning—like a tape playing over and over again. I heard the words I was speaking, knowing they were not my own. My voice even sounded different.

I was exhausted both physically and emotionally. Tom was having all he could do to keep from running out of the room. I give him credit for staying there with me. It was like seeing the aftermath of a terrible accident—hard to look at but even harder to look away.

I was unable to communicate anything other than this "message" that I'd been programmed with. It was one of the more strange things I endured in the course of my experiences. With great effort, I was able to say something other than that message, but it was only after I'd played it through three times. Eventually, I was also able to get up off the bed, but it was very difficult because my body felt so heavy and suppressed. I felt disoriented, like I'd vacated my body and given it over to another entity. Yet I was still in there, just no longer in control.

To some extent, I believe that is exactly what happened, but how that is possible I couldn't explain. They didn't hurt me physically even though I didn't look like myself. I looked like a "version" of myself. My husband was alarmed, and I kept looking into the mirror to find me in those eyes somewhere. "I" was cowering back in a corner of myself, hiding from the monsters that had come into our room and threatened me.

The message for Don was a vicious one. Basically, it said that they would no longer be allowed to regress me in order to retrieve memories and that Don had no idea what he was dealing with. They had been studying my family for generations, and the aspirations of a "small time" UFO investigator would not be allowed to interfere with their work. There was too much at stake. I delivered the message but was able to censor out some of the nasty condescending comments aimed at Don personally.

And true enough, when Stanley Mitchell tried to take me back to the repressed memories around the "Indian Angel" incident, I became almost hysterical. There was no way I was going to retrieve those memories. All I got was a message: they enhanced certain characteristics of my child's DNA.

That greatly disturbed me, and when I protested that they had no right to tamper with my child, I was firmly told, "Not tamper. We *enhanced* certain characteristics."

Later on when I reflected back on what the MIB's message had been, it caused me a fair amount of distress. They had said that my family had been studied for generations.

What did that mean? Had they been interfering with my ancestors? And what were the implications for my children— and their children?

The need to know if these beings were malicious suddenly took on a new meaning and urgency. I didn't have to think long and hard to remember some of the incidents from my childhood that seemed to support what they'd said.

UFO Sightings by My Mom

Late 1950s

I remembered a day in the mid to late 1950s when I came in from the outside to find my mother standing by the kitchen window looking intently out across the valley toward the hills beyond. I asked her for something, I don't recall what, but she didn't turn away from the window to answer me.

She kept searching out there as if looking for something. She answered in a vague way and sort of waved her hand at me as if to brush me away. I stood and watched her for a while as she alternated between sitting down in a chair and standing up, but she never turned away from the window or took her eyes off whatever it was she was looking at. It appeared she was searching because she would lean in and look to the west and then turn her head up to look at the sky.

Eventually I walked into the next room and sat quietly looking at books until my father came home from work. I don't know if they were even aware I was nearby as I heard my mother tell him in a very excited voice that she'd seen a flying saucer earlier that day hovering over against the hill across from our house.

I didn't know what a flying saucer was, but I knew it had to be something pretty special from the way my mother was talking about it. She was using a tone of voice that I'd never heard her use before, and my father was asking questions in a very controlled, calm manner. This made me scared. Something was up, and I slowly made my way back into the room.

When they saw me, they chased me away by sending me up to my room. I trudged slowly up the stairs and sat down halfway up in order to listen in to what they were saying, but they were now talking in whispers. That alarmed me even more.

That night at dinner I asked timidly what a flying saucer was, and I was given an explanation that was quite blasé. As the years rolled by, my mother never denied having seen a UFO, and she told how it had hovered over against the hills straight across from our house. Then it just shot up and was gone.

Spring 1966

She had another sighting years later. It was in the spring of 1966. My oldest brother was graduating from high school, and we were walking back to our house from the baccalaureate services when my mother suddenly stopped and pointed up above the treetops.

In a very excited voice she asked if any of us saw that thing in the air. "What is it? Do you see it?" she asked.

I looked but could see nothing. She was very agitated and anxious about what she was observing, as she stabbed her finger in the air, pointing. My younger brother was walking with us, and he claimed to see it, too. They described it as a metal tube-shaped object with a beam of light coming down out of the bottom of it almost to the ground. My mother saw something sliding upward inside the beam of light. I tried but could not see a single thing. I was frustrated by that, but being a teenager, I didn't really care much.

They stood and watched it for a few minutes until it disappeared. I never knew if it flew off or just faded away as I just gave up and continued the walk home. I admit that I doubted what they were saying although I knew my mother would never tell a lie. I simply thought she was mistaken about what she thought she was seeing. I always figured my brother went along with it just because. I mean he would have been about thirteen, so what did he know?

After an Eastern Star Meeting—1960s

As far as I know, those are the only two sightings my mother had, except I remember her telling the story about driving home at dusk from an Eastern Star meeting that had been held in a neighboring town. As she made her way home on the winding roads, it started to get foggy and then she saw the strangest thing.

An owl was standing by the road. I remember her telling this story because of how bewildered she was by the whole thing. She remembered being mesmerized by this owl and its large eyes. She also said it was white, pure white, and it just stood there and looked at her as she slowly drove by it.

I would suspect she had an abduction experience because the story ended with her being totally befuddled by the fact that she'd lost a couple hours of time and had no recollection of how that could have occurred. She rationalized it by saying that perhaps she'd gotten lost in that fog and wandered around for so much longer than she'd realized. This incident occurred sometime in the 1960s, but I really don't know when. My mother talked about it from time to time, but I never asked her to pinpoint the year it happened. It just didn't seem to be of any great significance. It was just one of those stories you hear growing up, and it stayed with me as she repeated it a few times and always with that questioning sense of bewilderment that accompanies those kinds of anomalies.

My "Impossible" Birth

Another story that my mother told me that had never impacted me too much but now was starting to cause me some concern may or may not be linked to UFO activity. It centered on my birth. Apparently, my mother had suffered a miscarriage approximately twelve months before I was born and because of that, she told me she never knew where I came from.

What she meant by that was that after the miscarriage, she abstained from any kind of sexual activity, and yet she found herself pregnant with me. I was born on Christmas morning in 1950, but according to my mother, my arrival should not have been possible. That strange phenomenon has shown up in my family at least one other time that I know of, so I am not the only person born under those strange circumstances. I can draw no conclusion that points specifically at the Greys' involvement, and yet, to a large extent I suspect there might be a link.

Being told that your family has been studied by a race of beings not of this world is a disturbing statement, to say the least. Having it come from those monsters, the MIB, made it an even more terrifying concept for me to accept. I found relative peace with it by taking solace in the fact that none of us seemed to be all that strange or unusual—well, unless you think me odd for writing this book. But as I continued to explore the events that had happened in my life and those that were now happening, I did find nuggets suggesting that all was not so terrible. That is, there were some good things that came from my interactions with the Greys. After all, I'd been given the opportunity to learn a great many things from them, the least of which were "The Three Important Things to Know."

*Your understanding is not an important contribution
to the truth.*

A Course in Miracles

Chapter 7:
Scattered Puzzle Pieces

Stigmata of Abduction Experiences

I had continued my association with the little group that
met once every week or so to meditate. They were helping me
to see my experiences from a totally different perspective, one
without fear. It was easy to feel safe and somewhat protected
while I was meeting with them, but when you wake up in the
morning with bruises on your arms or a swirling circular
pattern of flattened grass in the field next to your house along
with a faint memory of a silver ship sitting there—well, that
feeling of peace leaves very quickly. I was challenging the ETs
now, daring them to come during the day without putting me
into an altered state.

I was learning to meditate, and it seemed to somehow
open up a channel of communication with them. I didn't trust it
at first, and I questioned the validity of it for a long time, but
for sure I was starting to remember my encounters with them
without the aid of hypnosis, and I was also somewhat alert
when they came for me. It seemed they had always been a bit
reckless about "blocking" me early enough, as I had so many
conscious memories of them showing up at random times
throughout my life. Plus, there was that odd thing they do at
times; that is, they rap sharply three times before coming into
the room for me. I later learned that this is a common quirk of
theirs. I knew it meant they were there, but for some reason it
never frightened me; instead, it seemed to have a calming
effect on me.

There came a night when I was lying in my bed, trying to fall asleep when I became aware of a Grey's presence near the bed. I opened my eyes and wasn't even all that frightened to see him bending over me. I clearly recall that my left arm was under the covers, but my right one was outside, and I watched as he reached out and touched my arm.

I could almost say the words with him, "Sherry, it's time."

While the visits were traumatizing, I think the stigma associated with the whole phenomenon is even worse. I became very guarded and withdrawn after quickly realizing that this is not something that is easily accepted by others. It's all related to the "shame factor" I mentioned early on. I didn't talk to my closest friends about what was happening to me, and my family had pretty well withdrawn. I was no longer the self-confident person I'd been prior to all this showing up in my life. I was feeling a bit paranoid, and I no longer understood the world I was living in.

I had more than one person tell me that the talk around town was that I'd gone crazy. I was lucky that I'd never attached a lot of importance to what other people's opinions of me might be, so that didn't affect me much, but I had concern for my children.

My father also seemed to be worried about how this might be seen by others in the community. He told me that the president of the local bank had called him in and told him to talk to me—that I needed to get this whole UFO thing under control before it ruined my business. This definitely hit a nerve with my father, but I barely gave it a thought. At that juncture, I didn't care about my business. It was low on the totem pole of my concerns.

I became depressed, thinking that I was nothing more than a guinea pig for some other race of beings or a specimen that they were studying. Probably most of all, I was being forced to reconsider my place in the world and where I stood.

Where was God that something like this could go on?

And I had anger. Lots of anger. I directed it at the aliens but also at my family. In my mind, they had let me down. I remember being at a family gathering while the memories and bruises of an alien abduction that had occurred the night before were still fresh in my mind and on my body. I wanted to scream at them all to look—to listen to me—to understand that this was not my imagination running away with me. This was real, it was happening, and I needed them to care.

My meditation group became my family, as did sweet Marion from the CUFOS group. She didn't judge me or turn away from me. Sometimes that's all you need—just one person to hear you and accept you.

Order to Share Abduction Experiences—Late 1980s

One of the more unusual things that occurred during the 18-24 months of intense activity I experienced during the late '80s was a seeming order from the Greys to share my abduction stories with a handful of selected individuals. I was given a list of names and instructed to contact these people and talk with them about my experiences. Initially, I did not accept this as coming from the Greys. It was just too strange and didn't feel like something they would ask of me. It didn't make sense then, and it still doesn't make a whole lot of sense to me now. I resisted this request for a long time until I could no longer ignore it.

Let me try to explain how this request and subsequent compliance was experienced by me. It was experienced as a "pushing." That is, I don't recall Da or anyone verbally telling me to do this job; instead, it was just a knowingness I had along with a clear list of names. I recall there were about six people who were designated. I knew everyone on the list. Many were business associates; that is, they had done a real estate transaction with me, or they worked in a field that was compatible with my own. There was only one person on the list that I had any level of comfort about sharing my story with. The rest were all quite intimidating for me to think about discussing such an absurd subject with.

I cannot tell you how this frightened me. I tried so hard to convince myself that the idea came from somewhere within myself and could not have possibly come from them. I rationalized it away for as long as I could, but in the end, the "pushing" became intolerable. What happens is it becomes like an obsessive thought. It was interfering with my day-to-day activities and was becoming louder and louder. It's like I was being yelled at and the reminders to do this were making me crazy—or crazier.

Don't think I wasn't aware and am not now aware of how goofy this sounds. I've heard about the madman who walks into a business and shoots people at random all because a voice in his head had told them to. They believed it was God or the devil or some entity.

This *order* from them scared the crap out of me. You may find it hard to believe, but I really, really resisted doing this—not just because I didn't want to humiliate myself in front of these people but even more so because I didn't want to obey that seeming *order*. It was too similar to the defense given by the over-the-edge crazies who slaughter people because some voice told them to. I figured this was just a milder version of the same insane condition, and maybe this is how it had all started for those poor souls. But I eventually came to understand that when my guys want something, they don't back off. And there was no way I was going to get out of this assignment.

So I very, very reluctantly started to set up meetings with these people to have this terribly awkward conversation. I started, of course, with the woman I felt most comfortable with. We met for lunch, and I believe she expected our discussion to be about her property as I'd recently sold her home. I must say it turned into a very interesting conversation once I got over my initial embarrassment of bringing up such a taboo subject. It turned out her son was one of the children I later came to recognize as being a participant aboard the ship—he was a fellow abductee. This lady and I became fairly close and gave support to one another as we both struggled to find the meaning and purpose to these experiences. So that meeting was positive enough to encourage me to move down to the next name on the list.

The next talk went almost as well. This individual had been dealing with a sensitive issue that was tremendously difficult for her, and she viewed my offering to share such a private, painful subject as an opening for her to speak with me and thereby process some of her own hurts. We eventually became very close friends. I was starting to see that there might be a method to this madness. That is, there seemed to be a higher purpose to this whole agenda. I suppose the lesson could have been to simply get over myself.

Eventually, there was just one name left on the list, and it was a business associate that I respected so much that I simply could not bring myself to speak the words. I refused, but the pressure was almost painful. What happened was I found myself in this man's company one day when we were out looking at some land boundaries. He was a surveyor and did almost all the work that came through my office. We were in his truck, bouncing around looking at land, and it was the perfect opportunity to broach the subject.

It felt like my head was going to explode as "they" pushed and pushed on me to open up and start talking. I don't know if it showed—Lord, I'm sure it must have! It certainly felt like my whole head had expanded and he looked at me expectantly. Yes, it was like he knew I was going to say something, but I refused to allow it.

After that day, they let it go. He was the only one I didn't talk with, but I did live to regret it. I found out later that he had a high level of interest in the subject and had heard the stories about me. I guess he would have been very open to hearing what I had to say. It might have even given me some peace by his offering of acceptance and interest in the subject, but my pride had kept me from having that experience.

Lesson learned. Now I am very sad to report that this wonderful man passed away quite unexpectedly a few years later. I don't have many things in my life that I wish I could go back and change. I just don't harbor those kinds of regrets, but I wish I'd been able to overcome my own ego in order to share with him some of what was happening to me.

Again, I don't have a clue as to what that whole thing was about—maybe to get me comfortable with the experiences? Comfortable talking about them? Who knows? I don't spend time analyzing things anymore; turns out it's a waste of time. I accept that there was a purpose. Perhaps the benefactor was not meant to be me, but those I spoke with. I just wanted to include it in this story as I find it an interesting piece of the puzzle.

Missing Time During the Day

During this whole two-year period while these encounters were happening, I would experience missing time during the day. It would be random and very subtle—that is, there would be no sighting of a ship or any other red flag. Instead, time would simply be gone.

I remember driving along a main street in our village right after lunch. I was headed back to my office when all of a sudden I was in a completely different location, and the sun was no longer straight overhead. It was approximately three hours later than what it had just been. I was so shook-up, I pulled over to the side of the road and sat there.

It is a strange thing to try to explain, but even with everything going on with all the encounters and memories, I still sat there and tried to figure out what in the world had just happened.

I really didn't think, *Oh, it's them again. I must have just had an abduction.*

No, it's not like that. I sat there and tried to rationalize it to find an explanation. It didn't even occur to me for a very long time that I'd most likely just been abducted. Their blocking methods were that good.

General Confusion of Experiencing an Abduction

I will try to explain the general confusion you experience by putting it into these terms. Using my childhood abduction, the one where they took me above the planet and showed me the earth being destroyed, I would best describe it as being like pieces of a puzzle. You lay all the pieces of the puzzle out on the table. Most are face up, so you have a colorful piece of a picture, but because it's not connected to anything else, it doesn't make sense. It's just a pretty, colorful piece of something. Maybe you can make out a flower or part of a flower on the piece, but for the most part, it's gibberish.

The memory I had of my childhood incident was scattered just like that. There was a piece where I recalled being shown the earth being destroyed. I never forgot that scene, but I had no idea where I'd seen it. I knew without a doubt it wasn't a dream. I eventually came to think of it as a premonition I'd had, but I also had memories of Da standing behind me and speaking my name softly while I stood facing the gooseberry bush. I didn't know it was him, but I knew I'd had an experience where someone had come up behind me when I was out there picking berries on a very hot summer day. Then there was the eerie memory of my brother standing frozen in place on the sandstone rocks. That one was burned into my brain.

So those are three very clear memories—pieces of the puzzle, but I never connected the three pieces until after I'd been regressed. They didn't fit together until Stanley Mitchell had given me the suggestion to leave the door open so that I could recall other repressed abduction memories. It's a fascinating thing, but it was always a source of fear because it meant that I had secrets, a secret life that I didn't have any conscious recall of. I found that to be a very frightening concept.

Further Abductions

Surprise Birthday Party—Late 1970s

There is another incident that happened prior to my abduction memories coming to the surface. It happened in the late 1970s, and I think it's a good example of how powerful their blocks are. There was a party to celebrate my brother-in-law's birthday, and the party was being held at the bow hunter's clubhouse. This clubhouse is located just over the hill from the farm Vicky grew up on and just a short distance from where my roadside abduction had occurred in 1968. It was a full house as family and friends gathered for the festivities. We were instructed to be there by a specific time because it was a surprise party. As was typical for us, we arrived late but still in plenty of time for the celebration.

They had a live band and food. Since we didn't have much of a social life, I'd been really looking forward to this party. I wanted to dance, eat a little too much, and maybe drink a little too much! We arrived just as the band was setting up, and most everyone had already eaten, so we hit the buffet table, and I filled a plate to overflowing. I found a place to sit and was wolfing down my food while watching the band warm up when my sister-in-law came and told me I had to come outside and see something. I declined. I wanted to eat and be ready to dance as soon as the band played their first song.

Then she leaned down and whispered, "I think there are UFOs out there—you need to come and take a look."

Well, that intrigued me—remember this was pre-regression, before my memories had begun to surface. So I set my plate down, asked Tom to watch it, and went outside to take a look. There were other people out there—mostly children, and they were looking toward the south at some lights dancing around in the sky. It was hard to discern how many different crafts there might have been as the lights kept moving. As many as four or five red lights would appear at the same time, but they would move and dart around very quickly.

I didn't recall ever having seen anything like this. Because the aliens are able to block all the encounters and memories so well, I had no idea at this time that I'd ever seen any kind of UFO, much less been inside one.

I wasn't sure what to make of this—I was slightly disappointed because I wanted to see something more than just lights although they were definitely strange—no way could those be airplanes. I remember my sister-in-law asking me what I thought they were, and without taking my eyes off the dancing lights, I answered vaguely that they could be UFOs, but I didn't know.

I wanted to get back to the party, back to my food, and back to the dancing that was just starting—I could hear the band starting their first song. I turned to tell my sister-in-law I was going to go inside, but she wasn't there. Strangely enough, everyone who'd been standing with me watching the lights was now gone. I was alone. And it was quiet—there was no music. *How had everyone disappeared so quickly?* I looked around for them and called out my sister-in-law's name.

Then I realized that I wasn't standing out in front of the building, but I was somewhere else. I didn't know where I was. I was disoriented and confused by this odd turn of events. *Where was everyone? Where was I?*

I stumbled around, trying to get my bearings. I had been standing in a clearing by the road, but now I was surrounded by trees. I looked around and searched for something recognizable and noticed I was standing in tall grass and weeds on a wooded hillside. I caught a glimpse of the clubhouse lights below and moved toward them into an open area. I came out behind a shed and saw there were cars parked down below.

In a panic now, I quickly moved toward the cars and found our vehicle. I looked around. I was a good hundred yards from where I'd been standing only a second before. I felt my heart start to pound in my chest as I tried to make sense of this. In desperation, I yelled for my sister-in-law again and began sprinting toward the lighted building and what felt like safety.

I was disheveled. I tugged at my clothes as if to get them in place, and I tried to straighten my hair and put myself back in order. Somehow I knew I was a mess. I did my best to calm down before walking into the building. I went straight to my sister-in-law and demanded to know where she had disappeared to, but she looked at me like I was crazy. I was disoriented and frantic as I quickly moved away from her.

I went back to where I'd been sitting before being called outside, but my plate of food wasn't there. Everything was out of sorts. Something was wrong.

The band was packing up. Not only was my plate gone, but the food on the table was gone, and people were leaving—indeed, many had already left. My children ran to me and asked where I had been. They'd been looking for me—my youngest was very distraught, and Tom was furious that I'd skipped out on the party. He demanded to know where I'd been. I stood there in a total state of confusion and alarm. Panic was rising slowly in me as I hugged my youngest daughter and tried to calm her.

I was asking, "What happened? Why was everyone leaving? Did something happen?"

But Tom was in my face, demanding that I tell him where I'd run off to. I couldn't answer him, I didn't comprehend the question. I tried to explain that I'd gone outside to look at some lights in the sky, but then I just got quiet. I went numb. Clearly I was suffering from some sort of memory lapse, but what would cause that?

Did I have a stroke? Did I fall and hit my head?

Not one shred of a memory remains about what happened to me during that lost time. I'd been missing for well over two hours—maybe three! I never spent a lot of time trying to figure that one out. It scared me too much to look at it closely, but I can assure you that an alien abduction was not something that at that time I would ever have even considered. Now after all I've been through, it is clear that my guys were there and picked me up.

I think it's pretty daring that they came during a family gathering. Very bold of them. I also wondered about the proximity of this encounter to the one I'd had when I was 17. I seemed to have an idea deep in the recesses of my mind that there were certain areas where it was easier for them to enter our dimension. I wonder if my being in this location made it just too easy to pass up the opportunity.

The blocking that occurred with that episode was very deep as I'd been extremely upset about this situation, and yet by the time we got home that evening, I hardly gave any thought to the missing time or any of the other strangeness that had taken place.

Falling into Bed Abduction—Summer 1979

During this very same time frame—as a matter of fact, I believe it occurred within days of the birthday party abduction—I had what I think of as the "Falling into Bed" experience. My daughters were five and eight years old, and we'd recently moved into an old, ramshackle farmhouse that we were renovating. It was summer, and my husband had left for work earlier while the girls and I were still asleep in our upstairs bedrooms. What I remember is falling onto my bed very early in the morning. I'd been asleep but came awake at a point just below the ceiling and felt myself falling through the air for just a second before fiercely hitting the waterbed.

My youngest daughter had apparently climbed into my bed, and she went flying as my body slammed onto the mattress. We both squealed and grabbed ahold of each other to keep from bouncing onto the floor. At the same time, there was a very loud cracking sound as if a single thunder clap had occurred right in the room.

Then I heard my oldest daughter let out a scream from her bedroom down the hall, and she came running into my room. All in all, it was chaos. My little one was shrieking, and my oldest was rubbing her head and crying that she'd just fallen onto her bed and hit the back of her head on the headboard. I checked, and sure enough, she had a goose egg starting to form at the bottom of her skull. She was hurting from the bump but was even more upset by a disturbing dream she'd had—something about her dog, clowns, and being lost and unable to find her way back home.

I tried to comfort both of them, but my mind was racing with the facts and trying to make sense of it. I knew I had fallen into bed, and now here was my daughter saying the same thing. *How could that be?* I finally concluded that this old house must be starting to cave in and that we needed to get out ASAP.

I gathered up both of my girls and ran out onto the lawn with them. I searched the perimeters of the house for the place where the cave-in was starting. It seemed logical that it would be under my bedroom, but I could find nothing indicating any kind of structural compromise. I ran around the house, looking closely at the foundation, and finding nothing, knew I had to venture into the basement to look.

There could be no other reasonable answer to what had happened. Both my oldest daughter and I had experienced a sensation of falling into bed. The only thing that could cause that was for the house to drop out from under us. It could not possibly be anything else. My girls were starting to get worked up about being out on the lawn in their pajamas. They wanted breakfast, and I was looking with dismay and dread at the stairway into the basement.

I didn't want to go in there. What if the house fell in while I was down there? Not only could I be trapped, or worse, my daughters would be witness to that horrific event. I couldn't chance it. I took one more lap around the house, and seeing nothing of concern, we all went back in. I immediately went around the interior walls to see if there were any cracks or fusions. Again, there was nothing there.

I called my dad and explained what had happened. He told me straight up that it didn't make sense, but I was insistent. I knew what I knew. We had both had our beds drop out from under us, and my daughter had the goose egg on the back of her head to prove it. From what I'd experienced, I figured the floor had to have dropped at least four feet.

My dad finally agreed to come out and take a look at the house after we decided that maybe the gravel pit up the road had been put back into service, and perhaps a large dynamite explosion had shaken my house. It was a stretch, but it was all we could logically come up with.

I quickly got my girls something to eat and marched them back out onto the lawn to wait for my father. He arrived before too long and, bless his heart, he spent a lot of time looking and peering into places, even in the basement, but there was no evidence of any kind of collapse or foundation issues.

I discussed it with my husband that evening when he returned home from work. I was refusing to sleep at the house that night but didn't know where to go or what to do. He looked around the basement with a big flashlight, and still there was not one piece of evidence to support my story other than the nasty bump on our daughter's head.

I honestly don't recall if we stayed there that night or not, but once again, I was forced to just forget about the whole thing. There was no rational explanation for what had occurred, so I pushed it out of my mind although our oldest talked about the strange and disturbing dream she'd experienced for a good long while as it had upset her so much. I listened to her repeat that dream over and over again and no amount of comforting seemed to alleviate her anxiety.

These memories and many others were coming to the surface all during this summer of 1988—ever since the regression had taken place, and I'd opted to "keep the door open." There were times I regretted that decision, but when I'd made it, I really thought that all I was going to get was clarity about the 1968 roadside incident. I never, ever could have guessed that I'd been having these abductions throughout my entire life. And I certainly never expected to start having encounters that I would be consciously aware of.

Encounters of the Third Kind—Late 1970s

You must remember that I didn't even know such things occurred. An alien abduction story was as foreign to me as anything could be. And the reason for that is because they, they being the Greys, had kept me so blocked that I was unable to even comprehend the idea. Honestly, I remember Tom taking me to a drive-in movie in the late '70s. *Close Encounters of the Third Kind* was playing. At this time, I would have been about 26 or 27 years old, so I was having or had just had my own close encounter of a third kind when we were sitting there watching this movie.

Or, I will say, I *was trying* to watch it. What occurred for me was extremely strange and frustrating. I was seeing a screen that was completely jumbled, and the words were just as scrambled. None of it made sense to me. It was as if someone had taken the picture, cut it into dozens of pieces and put them back randomly. It was bizarre. I wanted to go talk to someone [about the mixed up screen], and I wondered why nobody else was complaining. I urged Tom to lay on the horn or at the very least, leave. I could not make out a single clear word or image. I kept asking Tom what was going on, as I couldn't for the life of me understand how anyone could comprehend it. It was so clearly messed up. Tom kept shushing me.

I finally got so frustrated I decided to go speak to someone about it. I marched into the concession stand and demanded to know why the movie was such a mess. How were we expected to watch it when it was so distorted . . . and the sound was just as bad!

The two young people working there looked at me like I had horns growing out of my head. Then they turned, looked at the screen, looked back at me, and said, "Lady, what are you talking about?"

I numbly stood there trying to comprehend the situation but couldn't stand the way they were staring at me, so I went back to the car, crawled into the backseat, and went to sleep.

It wasn't until a few decades later when I saw the movie on video that I was able to comprehend it. Now I understand why they didn't want me seeing it! There is a lot of truth in that movie. Someone knows something about the alien abduction experience up close and personal that they were able to write that screenplay!

Tom Moves On

It wasn't too long after the third hypnosis session and the encounter with the MIB that Tom moved out. It took a couple more years of on-and-off trying, but essentially our marriage was over. I think it was very hard for him, knowing he could not protect his family from these intruders. It was just easier for him to leave. I know he told people that I'd gone crazy and was hallucinating. I couldn't blame him; it was just his way of putting distance between himself and what was going on with me. Yet I believe he, too, could not rationalize away the events that were happening with increasing frequency.

Trying to Understand

Now I started with a vengeance to try to understand intellectually what was going on with these beings. I read books, I attended UFO conventions, and I went to local gatherings of people who'd had some sort of UFO experience. I also volunteered to help other "victims" of UFO abductions by going with the investigators and offering whatever comfort I could.

It helped me to be of help to others. Many times, the victims were children or young adolescents. The fear, bewilderment, and confusion associated with this phenomenon are astronomical. Trying to integrate the experience into your life and move forward with some kind of normalcy is virtually impossible. Sometimes the abduction would appear to be a one-time event, and other times like my own, it was a series of events occurring over a lifetime.

They did follow a certain pattern to some extent, and they always had a high level of strangeness about them—that is, the Greys. And it was almost always the Greys we were hearing about that would demonstrate such odd behavior as to make you question their intellect. Certainly, I had always thought they had to be a more advanced civilization since their technology was so far ahead of our own, yet their lack of compassion and basic understanding of what they were putting their "victims" through was unfathomable.

More than a few of my encounters ended with them dropping me from a high distance to the ground or floor below—like the farmyard incident! I could have frozen to death out there! It was things like that that confused me to no end. How could I believe they cared about my welfare when they did things like that? What about the bruises? The needle marks? The scars?

When I was very little, I'd only just been allowed to start taking baths alone, so how old is that? Maybe six or seven? I was obsessed with putting my little finger into a scoop hole that they'd left on my right calf. Funny, I knew what it was. I can actually recall sitting in the tub, placing the tip of my little finger in that scooped out indention and thinking about how they did it. It didn't hurt. They told me it wouldn't, and it didn't. It didn't even bleed; it just healed right over and left this little hole. I didn't really mind that they'd done it. They explained that it was necessary to make sure I was kept in good health. I had that little scoop mark for years and still have just the slightest scar from it.

It seemed the harder I looked for answers, the more confused I got. Finally, I realized the answers were not "out there." I could read all the books in the world, attend every lecture, every support meeting, every convention, and I would still come away with nothing but more questions. No wonder it is so easy to just say the abduction phenomenon is pure hallucination, dreams, night terrors, or fantasy.

Time to Regain My Power

The more I searched, the more frustrated I became. I decided to put my focus back on the meditation group. Oddly enough, both Don and the group were encouraging me to do pretty much the same thing in an effort to feel some sort of control over the events occurring. They were telling me I needed to take back my power.

After Tom moved out, my fear had become palatable. I was terrified of being at home alone. They were coming more and more frequently, and when I turned to Don for assistance, he said they could set up cameras, but that never deterred them, and no one had ever been able to capture anything on film. That didn't surprise me, knowing that they were of a different dimensional vibration, it would follow that we could not get their image on film. Many times, I would sense they were nearby, and I would go into a panic.

Once I found myself driving madly toward Madison in an effort to escape them. Suddenly, it was like I came awake as I realized that not only could I not hide from them, but my daughters were back at the house—alone. What kind of mother was I? I was out of my mind with fear; that's the kind of mother I was—fighting an enemy that couldn't be fought. I needed to go about this a different way.

I proceeded to challenge the Greys. First, I drove to a property I knew a few miles out in the country. It was an abandoned farm with a long, long driveway. The farmstead was isolated—no neighbors within sight. It was getting dark out. There was a shadow of a moon but no stars visible. I got out of my car and started talking to them.

It was a one-sided dialogue as I called them out and dared them to show themselves. I knew they were nearby, and I knew they could hear me. I walked down the lane and back again. My pleading escalated into crying and then ranting and raving as I shook my fist at them and called them cowards. I was fed up with living in fear. Tired of them sneaking in after dark and dragging me out of my home. Tired of what they'd done to my life—the devastation they'd brought down on me and the lives of my children. I wanted them to show themselves, explain why this was happening. Make it make sense to me. I looked up into the night sky and pleaded for an answer. They owed me that much, for all they'd taken from me. They were there. Why weren't they showing themselves? I cried and carried on for a good long while, walking up and down the road, kicking at the rocks, hitting my car with my fists, hurling insults at them, and venting all my anger and frustration until there was nothing left inside of me. I waited in the dark silence for a response. I halfway expected one. Spent with emotion, I crumpled to the ground, crying. I hugged myself as I rocked back and forth in the middle of that gravel road, and in a voice barely audible I kept asking, "Why?...why?"

I shut my eyes in order to see.

Paul Gauguin

Chapter 8:
Living with One Foot
in Another Dimension

Reclaiming My Home

A few nights later I did what was recommended by my group and Don. I went into every room of my home and declared it safe and off limits to them. I went outside in the dark and walked around my house without a flashlight or the benefit of a yard light.

I kept repeating, "This is safe. This is my home, and it's my safe space."

It was hard. When I started, I knew it was a lie—it most certainly was not safe, but I kept circling my house until it got easier, and the fear and doubt were replaced with a feeling of control and power. I felt the tightness in my chest and throughout my body let go as the heavy weight of fear lifted up and out of me. It was such a release it was staggering. I nearly collapsed with the sensation of it. That night I slept the most peaceful sleep I'd had in months.

There was a change after that. I entered into a new space that felt like I might have some say in what was happening to me—not the ability to stop the experiences from happening but more like I was fulfilling a contract I'd entered into a long, long time ago. An agreement I'd made to play this role and allow these experiences even though I didn't consciously remember it.

My perspective had shifted. The fear was not entirely gone—I wasn't sure it ever would be—but the cold, raw feeling of being a victim was lessening. There seemed to be a subtle change in their attitude toward me. Communication was opening up. I started to hear Da's voice even when he wasn't physically present. I was living with one foot in this dimension and another in their's. That's how it felt, and as I look back on those times, I believe that is a pretty good way to explain what was going on with me.

Meeting a Psychic Healer

It was right around this time that I took a dear friend of mine to see a psychic healer. She was suffering from MS, and we figured there was nothing to lose by trying this since her doctors hadn't been able to do much for her. The healing session was being held at the house of a spiritual teacher that I had recently met.

Soon after we arrived, the host invited my friend into a back bedroom for her session, and I was left sitting at the kitchen table alone when a man I didn't know came walking into the room. I later learned he was the healer. We nodded at each other as he walked past me to get a drink, but he stopped, stood still for a few seconds, and then backed up.

He looked at me intently and said, "My, you have a lot going on, don't you?"

I returned his gaze while I tried to decide if I should respond honestly or just give a polite answer.

But before I could say anything, he said, "You know you are barely here? You are essentially living in another dimension. You barely have a foot in this world."

I was dumbfounded. I told him that was exactly what it felt like.

"How do you know? Can you tell me what it's all about?"

He said, "Don't worry about your experiences. If you don't want them in your life, you don't have to have anything to do with them."

I asked the one question that had constantly bothered me, "Are they good or evil?"

He responded, "You will know what your function or role is when the time is right. You've been trained and taught by them your whole life. It's your life purpose. It's like you have a capsule in your head, and it's dissolving slowly to reveal all the information to you."

"But are they good or evil?" I asked.

He avoided the question again and said, "You're working with two different groups."

Then he turned away from me, got his drink of juice, and left the room.

I wanted desperately to talk more with him but knew that I'd gotten all the information he was willing to share. His insights were interesting, and I filed the experience away with all the other odd things in my life. I didn't dwell on it too much as it sounded strange and not likely to be the truth, based on my perspective at the time. However, as time went by, it appeared that his statement about the capsule dissolving was dead-on-center.

The part about them not having to be in my life never appeared to be true, but I've since come to understand why that is the case. As for my working with two groups, that still remains to be seen. As of this moment, I don't have any recollection of any other extraterrestrials but the Greys.

It was right at this time when I really was starting to feel as if I was gaining ground with the ETs and getting a sense of some sort of control and understanding—albeit minor—that I got the most devastating blow of all.

Discovering Daughter's Involvement—1988

I was standing in my kitchen one summer morning in 1988, finding any excuse I could to not to go into the office. I was numb with fatigue due to all the activity and overwhelmingly sad about the disintegration of my marriage. I felt defeated. I was leaning up against the island snack bar, trying to fortify myself for the day when down the hall came my oldest daughter. My heart ached with love as I watched this beautiful, delicate wisp of a girl come stumbling into the kitchen all sleepy-eyed.

She was dressed in her nightshirt, blonde hair all disheveled, and I couldn't help but reflect back on when she'd been a toddler. She always slept hard, and as was her habit, she was rubbing her eyes, trying to come awake.

I smiled at her as I asked what she was doing up so early—it wasn't really all that early, but for a 17-year-old during school vacation, it was early. She stated that she wanted to tell me about a dream she'd had—it was such a cool dream! She'd been taken by some men into a room and shown a whole array of pictures that were from her life. She became very animated as she told me about all the pictures she was able to see, and she went from one example to another, telling me about all these images that were not from a dream life but from her actual life.

I listened intently to her, and as she talked, I watched her walk over to the table—and that's when I saw them. The backs of her legs were all bruised—big round bruises—not small— but very large. I walked over and lifted up her nightshirt and sucked in my breath, as I saw the huge black and blue bruises on her back and upper thighs. I asked what had happened, who had she roughhoused with or what had she been up to that would result in these horrible bruises.

She was oblivious. She was now saying that these same men in her dream had quizzed her on the things she was supposed to be learning, and they'd told her she was not doing as well as they'd like. She was genuinely upset about that. It was important she learn these things the men had told her, but she just wasn't getting it. Now she was getting agitated.

I was trying to listen to her, but I was sickened by the bruises and wanted her to tell me how they had gotten there. Again, she was very dismissive of them. I was deeply disturbed by what I was seeing and somewhat alarmed by the dream she was recalling. If I could get a rational explanation of the bruises, it would be easier to dismiss the dream as just that, a dream. Together, the two painted a picture I didn't want to see.

I examined the nasty bruises closely. It seemed clear that this was not something that could happen from her just bumping into something or someone. They were on her *back*. It didn't make sense—how does one get bruises all up their backside like that? It looked like someone had taken a small wrecking ball and hit her full force with it.

I checked the rest of her body and found nothing else. I stopped pressing her for answers. I could tell she wasn't hiding anything from me. She was focused on the disturbing dream, and these bruises were not concerning her in the least.

I was trying not to see the obvious, and I might have been able to let it go, but soon after, I was forced to see it for what it was. Too often now my daughter was sharing with me events that had the bizarre nature and trademark of encounters with the Greys. I had been very careful to keep my experiences from the girls, but it was impossible to protect them entirely from all the activity and strange things going on at our house. I kept trying to tell myself that it was just her overactive imagination, or maybe she was seeking attention. That would have been understandable as I'd been so distracted by all I was dealing with that certainly both my daughters had paid a dear price. But she was exhibiting fear—deep fear.

And that was not something that would be present if she was just letting her imagination carry her away. Also, her stories had the high level of strangeness that is associated with the whole UFO abduction scenario. Add to this that a few of her friends had been witness to some of these odd events, and it was all too clear that something was amiss. It pained me to see her confusion and anxiety escalate, but I continued to watch and observe, not wanting to believe it was really happening to her.

The answer came one night when I awakened with a sickening knowingness that my daughter was not in her bed. It was only my strong love and feeling of protectiveness for her that gave me the ability to awaken fully from the deep state of sleep I was in. So deep was this state that it reminded me of a drug-induced sleep like anesthesia.

I now know that I was not meant to come fully awake because as I did, that horrible feeling of fear for my child brought clarity to my senses, and I jumped out of bed and ran down the stairs to her room. She was not there. The covers on her bed were turned down very neatly, as if she'd gotten up and straightened them behind her. The sick feeling in my stomach escalated into panic. What to do—who to call—where to go? I forced myself to be rationale—this may not be what it looks like. After all, she was a teenager, and I had to consider the possibility that she'd sneaked out of the house to meet her boyfriend.

So I went back upstairs to my room and sat on the bed. I'd had good luck with the strong ESP powers I'd developed while spending time in the company of my guys, so I put them to the test once again. I projected myself "out" to go in search of my daughter, and I quickly found her crumpled up on the floor, back up against the wall in an altered state of consciousness. I recognized the situation—she was with the Greys.

I immediately panicked. I started to call out for Da and demand that he bring my baby home safely—NOW. I was furious as I continued to yell out to him.

Finally, I calmed down enough to hear his response that yes, she was there with him, and they would be bringing her back soon. She was fine.

I demanded to know what they were doing with her. *Had those bruises been caused by them?*

"She is part of the program; you know that," came his response.

"No, that is not allowed. Take me as much as you like but leave my child alone," I demanded.

"That is not possible," he stated without emotion.

I argued, cursed him, and pleaded with him. I begged and I bargained. Nothing I said had any impact on him whatsoever. When it was clear that I had no say, no power, no possible way to protect my child, I asked if they could at least treat her gently.

Did he know she was being brought back with bruises covering her body? They were handling her too roughly! Did he know she was living in fear—tormented by partial memories and "dreams" of them quizzing her, demanding she learn certain things.

"If you can't leave her alone, at the very least you need to promise me you will be gentle with her and let no harm come to her. **And block her!** Block her so well that she never will have to go through what I've gone through. Block her so she never has an inkling of what is happening to her. Can you do that?" I pleaded.

He said he would. It was little consolation.

I initially suffered deep guilt over this situation. It came from the belief that I had somehow brought this down on my child—that because of my involvement with the Greys, I'd somehow opened the door on this activity, thereby allowing it into my child's life.

And I couldn't protect her—that is the most helpless feeling in the world. There was nothing in my experiences up to this point or after that even came close to the trauma and pain I felt from learning of her involvement. I couldn't protect my child. I was then terribly afraid to go to bed at night.

How could I close my eyes and sleep when they might be coming for her?

The fear I'd experienced when I knew I was their target was nothing like this. It wasn't even close.

I would have done anything to keep her safe, and my mind raced as I tried to find ways to make that happen. I talked to Don about it, and he said I could put her in a sealed concrete bunker miles below ground, and they would still get to her if they wanted to. There was no way to keep the Greys away or stop these abductions from occurring. I felt like I was going to go mad with the helplessness of the situation.

Of course, I knew there'd been clues as to her involvement with the Greys prior to this experience, but the memories were so new and had been coming at me so fast and furious, I hadn't really had time to take it all in and get a clear picture. It had all been so overwhelming. I was still sorting through my own experiences with them and analyzing what I knew for sure and looking for meaning and purpose. It had been too much and really, I have to admit, I didn't *want* to see this. It changed everything.

The memory of what the MIB had said came rushing back at me. They'd said this "study" of my family had been going on for generations, and it was too important for it to be spoiled by my having it come into my awareness and under the scrutiny of a "small time" UFO investigator. This new revelation shot a great big hole in the recently acquired sense of peace that I'd obtained from declaring my home safe. This put me back to square one, and my anger escalated beyond anything I'd experienced up to this point. It consumed me.

As time went by, it was clear that there were many, many incidents that involved my daughter, but I will not be telling her story. I was very reticent to include anything at all about my children, and I refused to do so until it became too obvious that I was omitting a big piece of the puzzle. This will remain primarily the story of my involvement with the Greys, but certainly the story of my daughter's involvement overlaps with my own. If either of my children have anything more to say, it will be on them to come forward. I will not speak for them as this is too highly personal of a subject. I only know that Da seemed to live up to his end of the bargain.

One day about a week after my daughter had gone missing in the middle of the night, I was sitting out on our back deck when she came out and sat down next to me on the step. At one point, as we talked, she stretched out her arms in front of her and then turned them over. She was innocently stretching and rubbing her arms when I saw the distinct bruises of the Grey's fingers on her forearms where they'd gripped her. My stomach lurched as I fought the urge to grab her into my arms in a belated effort to protect her. I struggled to stay calm as I watched her rub her hand up and down her forearm. She was talking about what she'd done the night before when I observed her notice the bruises.

She didn't panic as I feared she might but looked at them, squinted, looked closer, and then said, "Hmmmm, I wonder how I got these?"

Then she went back to her story. I was relieved and somewhat amazed that she didn't connect the dots but was sad beyond measure that the proof of what was still happening to her was there on her body. For the most part, her blocking has remained very strong, so the fear she exhibited has dissipated. For that at least, I am grateful.

Needing Down Time—Summer 1988

It was now the late summer of 1988, and I was exhausted. Everything had gotten to me. I could hardly function, so for the first time in my life, I took two full weeks off from work. I stayed home and rested. Trying to function at a job where I had to interact with clients in a professional manner had reached the breaking point for me.

I remember being out with some people and walking around their home. They were planning to list their property with me, and they were showing me the boundaries of their lot, but I was distracted by my memories of an encounter I'd had one or two nights before. I was trying to fill in the missing pieces, and I kept pushing up my sleeve to look at the bruises they'd left on my forearm. At one point, while we were standing by their garden, I checked again.

Yup, still there. I hated seeing them as they were a visual *in-my-face, no-disputing* reminder of what was happening to me. I would do that. Go back and take another look over and over again always hoping that I had been wrong—maybe exaggerating or somehow making a bug bite into the dreaded markings of their vise-like grip.

I looked at the couple and tried to focus. They were proudly telling me about their orchard and their plantings. I could feel myself slipping. It was welling up in me—the anger and frustration. I resented these people for having such a neat and tidy life—a normal life!

I wanted to shout at them, "Who cares about your damn trees?! Don't you see we have bigger issues to deal with! Explain to me how aliens can come into my home and take my child? You don't believe me? Well then, explain these bruises to me! You see the aliens left these on me when they dragged me from my bed last night! Explain *that* to me, huh!"

That was when I knew I needed some down time. I was going to blow one of these days, and that would not be good.

Driving Incidents # 1 & 2

The Drive Through—1979

Right around this same time I started to have a very strange thing happen while I was driving. At almost every intersection I would come to, as I pulled out, I would hear a deafening crash like I'd been hit hard by another vehicle. It was extremely unnerving, and I couldn't figure out how to make it stop. My mother was with me once when it happened, and I asked her if she heard it. She hadn't.

As I talked to her about it, I actually became aware that at some point it had been explained to me why this was happening. I'd had several fender benders since this whole UFO stuff had started happening, so the crashing sound was a reminder to be extra-extra cautious in order to get me through safely. I was distracted by all that was going on with me, and I was definitely accident-prone. That I agreed with—keeping my focus was becoming very difficult. This crashing business went on for several weeks, and during that time I had a very strange thing occur.

I was sitting at the main intersection of the entrance to our village. The highway that skirts along our community is a somewhat busy one, and this day I was coming back into town from my home and needed to cross that highway. I stopped, looked both ways, or so I thought I did, but when I pulled out into the middle of the intersection, I saw with horror that a big beige sedan was headed right for me. He was coming fast. I looked at the driver as he closed in on me.

Damn, he was going to catch me straight on.

My fingers tightened on the wheel instinctively as I pushed down on the accelerator, but I knew it was hopeless. I watched him and his passenger come toward me. I saw the fear on their faces as they, too, realized what was about to happen. I didn't look away as I braced for the crash.

Then there was silence. No crash.

What happened? Where had he gone? He simply wasn't there. I was still in the intersection, had been watching him closely, but now he was gone—just gone. I was only halfway through—basically blocking both lanes. It didn't make sense.

I quickly turned and looked the other way. There he was— driving away. That beige car was driving away and still in his own lane. I couldn't comprehend it. It was not possible.

Could he have somehow swerved around me and managed to get back into his lane without losing control of his car? Could he have done all that without me seeing it happen? Was there even room for him to do that?

The answer to all those questions is a definite *no*. When I turned and saw the car driving away, it was right there—not a quarter mile down the road but *right there*.

Clearly, he had somehow driven right through me, but my mind rejected that solution altogether. I looked at the face of the guy sitting at the stop sign and tried to read his expression.

Had he seen what happened? He must have.

Many, many times I thought about going to that guy and asking him what he had witnessed. He was a local man, and I certainly could have, but I never forgot the way he looked. He was staring straight ahead without any kind of expression whatsoever—almost with a dream-like look on his face. I didn't have to ask him. I think I was pretty certain what his response would have been.

Truth be told, this wasn't the first time I'd had an experience of this sort, and it wasn't the last. Evidently, I have very good angels watching over me. Or is it them—the aliens protecting their specimen?

Unassisted Sharp Turn—1979

When I was 29 years old, I worked in downtown Madison and made the 30-minute commute every day. Anyone who knows me knows I like to drive fast—always have and still do. One morning I was driving my new Pontiac Grand Prix to work, taking my usual route, which consisted of back roads— shortcuts that allowed me to drive faster than the speed limit. As always, after heading down a long, gentle slope, I had a decision to make. At the bottom of the hill where it leveled off, there was an intersection. I could continue straight ahead, or I could turn left. Either way got me to my destination.

I was going at least 65 mph as I came down that hill, so even though I'd sorta planned on making the turn, I decided at the last second since I was going so fast, to just go straight. But that's not what happened. At the bottom of the hill right when I reached the intersection with the road I'd decided not to take, my car suddenly and very abruptly slowed down.

I'll never forget the sound of the radio as it changed—it sounded a lot like when you put your head under water. The announcer's voice went "eeerrruuppp" and became deep and ridiculously slow like a tape that had broken and was rolling to a stop. I didn't have much time to try to take all this in because now the car was starting to turn. I looked at my hands on the steering wheel—and this I will never forget because it was so outlandish—but my hands never moved the wheel. They stayed exactly in the exact same position they'd been in—my right hand at the top of the wheel and my left hand lower on the wheel as my elbow was on the armrest of my door.

A car was sitting at the stop sign, and there was a lady in it. I turned my head toward her, but it happened in slow motion.

I tried to scream at her, "What's going on?"

But instead, my mouth formed the words very slowly, and they sounded like the announcer's on the radio. Slow—very, very slow—and deep. It would have been funny had it not been so damn strange and frightening. The sensation of the whole event was as if a giant hand was on my car and turning it, much like I used to do with my toy cars.

It was always frustrating to me as a child that the front wheels of the toy cars didn't turn, so you'd have to angle the car around the corners of the make-believe roads. That was exactly what this felt like—I was being maneuvered around the corner, but my car wasn't really involved any more than I was! Then, when my vehicle was completely around the corner and on the straightaway, it was released from whatever had a grip on it. The radio sped up to normal sound, and my car immediately zoomed up to the speed I'd been going before. My body was pushed back against the seat as it was so sudden.

I quickly hit the brakes as I had the intention of going back to talk with the lady sitting at the stop sign before she got away. I wanted to know what she'd seen. I glanced into my rearview mirror to make sure she was still there, and that's when I noticed it. Movement alongside the road.

I swung my head around and looked out my passenger window, and my heart started to pound at what I saw there. A train was racing down the tracks! What? Those railroad tracks were in use? I'd had no idea. I turned around and looked at the intersection to see if gates were down, but there weren't any! Not only were there no gates, but the train was well into the intersection—actually the engine was already past. Had I gone straight, I would have barreled into the side of that train going 65 mph. I would have been dead.

I pulled off to the side of the road. My hands were shaking and my insides churning. *My precious babies would be motherless;* that's all I could think.

I was shook-up all day and could barely function at work. At one point I started to go to my supervisor to tell her what had happened but realized how crazy my story would sound. I obsessively played it over and over again through the day.

Eventually, I got angry. Why was it that there was no sign, no warning of any sort at that crossing? A few days later I made some calls and tried to report it to someone, but I remember feeling helpless about not finding anyone who seemed to care.

There was not one day that went by for at least two and possibly three years where I didn't think about that incident. It was a mystery to me. I wondered how it happened. Who or what made it happen, and I wondered why my life had been spared. I didn't tell too many people about it. I'm not even sure I mentioned it to my husband. It felt too sacred. Talking about it seemed to trivialize it, and I guess I wanted to keep it between me and God for a while.

I had another amazing incident as I drove through the Arizona desert in 2008, and I will share that with you in a later chapter. It was just as dramatic and just as clear, but again it wasn't my time. I do remember telling someone that if there is an upside to the whole alien contact thing, it is that you are being watched over and protected.

Yes, they take you onboard their crafts and do strange and intrusive things to your body, but the flip side appears to be that they won't allow you to get sick, not anything serious. And on top of it, they teach you self-healing techniques. Clearly, they don't want you going and dying before they are done with you—at least that's been my take on it all. I liked it better when I thought it was an angel or God saving me from my wicked driving, and maybe it is, but my bet is on the Greys.

The first and greatest commandment is
don't let them scare you.

Elmer Davis

Chapter 9:
Please, Just Put Me
in a Padded Room

Lessons Begin—Fall 1988

Living through the multitude of visits from the Greys was just plain exhausting—not to mention frightening, bizarre, unnerving, shattering, and life-challenging. It was September of 1988, and my abduction memories had been uncovered for only five months. It had been a rapid deterioration of my life. I no longer felt safe anywhere. I had constant concern for my children. My marriage was pretty much over. My relationships were strained. My reputation in my community was tarnished. My grasp on reality and what I had always considered to be the truth was washed away. I felt I had nowhere to turn for help. It is difficult to find the words to explain just how much of a struggle it was to go out into the world every day and present a normal face while you are having these extremely strange things occurring in your life.

Meanwhile, my relationship with the guys had started to change, and I was becoming more and more aware of their contact. That fall of 1988, they started a "training" process with me. It wasn't clear to me at the time that I was being prepared to fulfill some role or function they had planned for me. I only knew that I was spending so much time with them that I was starting to feel like an alien in my own world.

Illusion of Time—The Sequential Time Incident

They started by teaching me about the illusion of time. According to them, time does not exist; only the measurement of time is what makes it appear real to us. We think that because we have a device (a clock) that appears to break the eternal "now" moment into seemingly separate "now" moments that it somehow means time is real. It is not. We created time, and we can control time, such as it is.

This lesson went hand in hand with their continuing discussions about the power of our minds. To prove to me that time does not exist, they started to make "waves" with my time. That is, I started to experience timelessness. When it started, to get my attention, the clocks would always be in sequence, no matter when I would check it. I would awaken at night with a strong urge to look at the clock, and it would be 1:23 or 2:34 or some other sequential number. Sometimes it would go backwards—4:32 seemed to be a favorite of theirs. Not for a solid four or five days could I catch the clock not being in sequence—ever. And I tried. This just about pushed me over the edge. It actually went on for over three weeks where I rarely looked at a digital clock without it being in sequence. That's a long time, and it was beginning to feel like torture.

I recall one day during this training when I was sitting at my desk, waiting until I was absolutely certain that it was not close to 12:30 before leaving for lunch. The 12:34 sequence had been particularly intense of late, and I knew if I saw it one more time I would go completely mad. I tentatively watched the wall clock in my office, which was an old-fashioned clock with hands. I waited until it was at least 12:45 before walking out to my car for the drive home.

Now the day before I'd left early, about 12:15, thinking I would miss the dreaded 12:34 sequence, but it had been there on my digital car clock, as always. So I figured I was going to be pretty safe leaving this late. Still, I did my best to avoid looking at the clock in my car, and I made it a few blocks, but again I looked. I remember exactly where I was—sitting at the stop sign by the post office, and in spite of my best effort I glanced down at the clock. You may be wondering how this is possible—how I could not control such a simple thing.

But I would respond to that by pointing out that that was the least of my concerns. I couldn't control any aspect of what was happening to me, much less this seemingly minor thing. They wanted me to learn something, so I was going to learn it. End of discussion.

I laughed a bitter laugh when I saw the 12:34 green digital numbers on the clock. I really wanted to cry, to scream, to run. But truth be told, I was fairly well beaten down by this point and had only enough energy to allow a sarcastic laugh.

I drove the quick five-minute commute to my house and pulled into the garage. I stayed in the car. I refused to get out. I knew what waited for me in my kitchen—two more digital clocks. I knew where all the digital clocks were by now. So I stayed where I was for a full five minutes. Then I got out and walked out of the garage and across the backyard to my small garden. I spent at least another ten minutes pulling weeds and picking a few tomatoes and peppers. As I walked toward my back deck, I knew I would see the digital clocks upon entering, but I also knew it was not possible for them to be in sequence. It was way past 12:34, and it was not yet 1:23. I felt like I might have broken the curse.

I came in the patio door and walked through to the kitchen with no fear. I was so positive I was safe. My armful of vegetables fell to the floor as I stood staring at the clocks. They both said 12:34. Of course it was impossible, but that didn't matter.

This tampering with time seemed to go on forever. It became so distracting to me that I begged them to stop. And then I threatened to kill myself if they didn't. I know that it does not sound like it would be such a horrible, terrible thing to endure, and yet it was. Maybe it was the straw that broke the camel's back, or maybe it was just the pure lunacy of it. I do know that it was a constant reminder of what was happening to me. There was simply no escaping it.

How many times a day did I check the clock?

And I was waking up at night at least once but usually more with a compulsion to check the time. I think it was the unrelenting nature of the experience that drove me to distraction and made me feel so out of control. I did not, while going through the experience, understand what it all meant.

I talked with my group about it, and we speculated that perhaps certain sequential numbers were meant to trigger a pre-set emotional response in me as we knew they were studying the human and all its attributes, but that never resonated with me as the only emotional reaction I had was frustration and anger.

The Slowly Dissolving Pill of Remembrance

The clarity about what it all meant came years later. The lessons seemed to be buried very deep, but eventually they would work their way to the surface, and I would find myself "remembering" certain things I'd been told. Again, I would not always know who, what, or where I'd been told this information, but I would embrace it as truth even though it would appear seemingly from out of nowhere and sometimes be radically counterpoint to what my previous belief had been.

It's a hard thing to describe, but that's how it appears to work. It's like they put a tablet in my mind—a tablet like an aspirin—and it dissolves very slowly over the course of your life, and the information contained within the tablet seeps into your brain or awareness and becomes known to you. It almost feels as if you've always known and understood this piece of information, but you know you haven't, at least not on the surface, and yet there is a sense that it was there—just buried very deep. It seems to have worked on this time issue because I eventually came to understand the lesson, which was that neither time nor space exist, and that we really do have the ability to control it.

Increased Intuition and Healing Ability

They'd always told me that our bodies were at the command of our minds and that it was an easy process to heal any ailment we might be convinced we were suffering from. I'd actually always had conscious memories of doing a few self-healing episodes on myself by following the techniques they had taught me. What I never knew, at least prior to my regressions, was *who* had taught me that method.

During this period of time while my involvement with the Greys was so intense, I noticed that my intuitive side, as well as my ability to heal, were both augmented a great deal. I also found that I could "hear" people's thoughts. It seems intrusive, but it really didn't feel that way to me. It was quite startling the first time it happened. It was different than getting an impression of what someone was thinking based upon their facial expression or demeanor. I literally "heard" the person's voice in my head as if they had spoken out loud.

Their visits were very intense throughout the entire year of 1988 but especially during the summer and into fall. I was experiencing missing time during the day, as well as having visits during the night. I developed a love/hate relationship with them. I was extremely frustrated that their visits had to be so covert, and I communicated to them that I wanted them to come to my home on a Sunday afternoon, ring my doorbell, and come in and visit with me properly.

Their response was that they could not do that. The vibrational differences required that I be put into an altered state while in their presence for any length of time. And that I was not as prepared emotionally and mentally as I seemed to think I was to have them show up at my front door. The fear factor was still high.

Let me explain what I mean when I say that I asked them to come to my house and that they responded. The mind-to-mind communication that went on when I was with them was also available to me at times when I could not physically see them. But there were definitely times when I knew they were very close, and I got pretty good at noticing the signs. The air around me would seem to tingle, and there was that strong sixth sense awareness of their presence.

I was also "hearing" Da speak to me at random times. The first time it happened I was driving down my driveway, and his voice came from behind me. I slammed on the brakes and spun around in my seat expecting to see him. This episode happened early on in the spring and was probably meant to comfort me, but it had the opposite effect.

What he said was simple: "Sherry, remember you are special."

My reaction was one of anger and frustration, and I responded by shouting, "You bastard! Don't patronize me!"

I waited for a response, but none came. So into the silence I said, "Just leave me and my family alone."

I continued to sit in the driveway while I tried to compose myself. I thought about how familiar his voice was to me and how I'd heard it so often throughout my life—especially when I was a small child. I started to regret my harsh response. Many times I would reflect back on that incident, wishing I'd reacted differently.

What if I'd been calm and responded in a civil manner? What kind of conversation might we have had? What might I have learned? Certainly I could have asked questions or gained insight into what was happening to me.

I'd been begging them to treat me in a conscious, civil manner rather than putting me into an altered state, yet when he does, I become hysterical. It was against my nature to be that way, but given the limits to which I'd been pushed, I don't think it was a totally unreasonable reaction.

Thundering Footsteps Incident

It was during the period of the sequential time incidents that I had a very odd interaction with them. It was a Friday afternoon, and I was home alone. I knew they were nearby, and I started to feel quite anxious about it. I paced back and forth, knowing they were planning one of their visits later that night. I stepped outside onto the bedroom balcony that faced the wooded hillside behind our house and immediately felt them out there watching me. I swear I really could smell them this time.

They do sometimes have a unique odor. Not always, but it was there at times. It reminds me of when I was a child, and in the autumn I'd push all the fallen leaves into a pile and bury myself in them. That is what they smell like—damp fall leaves, but with a little scent of spice added. So I peered into the woods and scanned the hillside as best I could. I half expected to see their silver ship sitting somewhere in the trees or hovering above the treetops.

I quietly said, "I know you're there."

Silence. But I felt them move closer.

Again, a little louder, I said, "I know you're out there, you cowards."

Nothing. Now the hair on the back of my neck started to tingle—they were very close.

So again, "You're cowards—that's what you are! Look at me! You're afraid of me! You have to wait until I'm asleep before you come creeping into my room to drag me from my bed. You cowards!"

The trees rustled as if in answer.

I continued my tirade, my voice escalating, **"Cowards!"**

I started to laugh. I was acting insane, I knew, but it felt good to be the tormentor instead of the tormented. I felt empowered. I knew they were out there watching me, and I knew they could hear my challenge. I stopped to listen and looked intently into the trees, wanting but not wanting to see them.

Everything was calm, and there was a faint breeze. The hair on my arms stood up, and I became very uneasy. I moved into the house and perched cross-legged on the bed, facing the wooded hillside. I laughed a nervous laugh and continued my harassment.

Suddenly there was a loud crashing sound. I froze.

What the hell was that?

Again it came—the sound of huge footsteps—that's the best way to describe the destructive sound that had started out in the trees. It sounded as if a massive animal was making its way through the woods.

I remember thinking, *Even an elephant wouldn't make that sound. This would have to be a gigantic dinosaur.*

I peered out into the trees, fearful of what I was going to see, but all was calm. And yet the sound continued. It, whatever *it* was, was getting closer as the thundering sound escalated.

I laughed at the absurdity of it. I wasn't about to let them win this battle. I loved how it had felt—that feeling of control, and I wasn't about to give it up easily. I knew they wouldn't hurt me. It was just a sound—they were creating it, It was harmless.

I started my tirade again as I yelled above the ruckus, "I'm not afraid! You're the cowards."

This went on for some time. I couldn't really tell you accurately how long, maybe as much as three to five minutes. It was amazing how loud the crashing sound got. I was sure I would soon see trees toppling over as the sound was so thunderous and destructive. I jumped off the bed and looked out, trying to see where they were, to see what was happening. I couldn't believe there was no change in the landscape. I dived back onto my bed, determined to hold my ground.

Now the sound grew even louder so that it started to reverberate within me. It permeated everything. It felt like it was beating against my body, shaking the house on its foundation. It was deafening.

Suddenly, it dawned on me what I was up against.

What was I doing taking these guys on? Was I crazy?

I toppled over on the bed and covered my head while pleading with them to stop.

"You win," I said meekly. "You win!"

I *felt* them smile.

New Series of Lessons

Soon they began a new series of lessons. The sequential time lessons had included the idea that time and space were an illusion, as well as reinforcement of lessons they'd given me my whole life on the power of the mind and The Three Important Things to Know. They don't teach you in the same manner as we are taught in school by an instructor. As I explained previously, they somehow drop the information into your head, much like a computer that is downloading a new program. But there are times when they expand on the newly downloaded program by giving details and examples.

These examples come in the form of *experiences* (such as the sequential clock ordeal) that are there to simply reinforce what they are trying to convey to you and *demonstrations* of what is being given to you in the form of "knowingness." These are illustrations and/or visionary supports of what it is you are learning. The "nuts and bolts" of what they want you to know is simply put into your mind through the download process. That is why you seem to remember something you learned but do not always have a clear memory of when or under what circumstance you learned it.

Many, many times I would only know I'd been given new information when I would hear myself start to explain something that I'd previously had no knowledge or very limited knowledge about. One of the oddest things I ever heard myself tell a friend was the fairly detailed workings of the typical flying disc. I used words I didn't even know existed as I went on for a good long while giving intricate details of how they operate. It was interesting, and it all made perfect sense to me at the time although I'm not sure I could bring that information to the surface now with such clarity.

Light Readings

In retrospect, learning to be a "light reader" turned out to be my most favorite lesson from them. Again, at the time I was going through it, I was in such a confused and fearful state that I regret I may have missed the opportunity to get more out of the experience. It came right on the heels of the sequential time incidents, and it enchanted me, scared me, intrigued me, and bewildered me all at once.

I was at my desk doing paperwork early one weekday morning when an older gentleman and his wife walked in to ask some questions about real estate. He was very vibrant and youthful, as was his attractive wife.

I stood up to greet him, and as I extended my arm to shake his hand, I looked into his eyes and immediately got the message "You will be staying."

I had the strongest urge to say it out loud but restrained myself. I then greeted his wife, and as I looked into her eyes, I got the same message. I could "see" their light and knew their "light reading" was high. So they would be staying. Staying where, I didn't seem to know at that moment, and I made myself focus on what they were saying.

They were asking questions about the real estate market, general questions that I answered easily, and then out the door they went.

I immediately thought, *What was that all about?*

To my surprise, I got a response.

I instantly "remembered" Da explaining to me that I would be doing light readings for two half-day sessions just to give me a run through of what it would be like should the need arise for me to do them in the future. He had explained that I would actually see the vibrational energy of the person's spirit and the higher the vibration the higher the light reading. Those with higher readings would be allowed to stay, and those with lower light readings could not be allowed to stay.

"There is no judgment of good or bad in any of this," he stressed. "Those with low light readings just need more time to develop and learn their lessons. The positive and negative have moved too far apart; they can no longer occupy the same space. Think of it as the ends of two magnets being brought together."

And as he said this, an image of two magnets repelling each other was shown to me.

"See how the positive and negative cannot occupy the same space? So it is with humanity. There are many who are at the level where they are ready to live in peace and harmony with the planet and other sentient beings. But there are those of the lower vibration who still believe war and violence are necessary. Their lessons will need to continue until they also reach the higher vibration, which they will as all must evolve."

I stood by my desk, taking all this in, fascinated by what I was learning—or remembering.

Da continued, "There isn't much time left, and it appears humanity will not reach the tipping point although it could happen. If enough humans reach a certain level of vibration, it has the effect of pulling those of a lesser vibration up. Humanity will not be allowed to destroy themselves or hold the planet back *again*. Therefore, if you don't reach the saturation level, each and every human being will be given the choice to stay or leave the planet. It is an absolute truth that the earth will be moving into the higher vibration, and those unable to survive that shift because of their lower frequency will be taken to a new place to continue their growth at their own pace without interfering with the earth's evolution or their fellow human beings' right to live in peace."

I was amazed. The enormity of it all overwhelmed me, and I was also fearful.

Just when was this deadline for humanity? How would people be taken off the planet? Would spaceships come and gather up families—maybe some members of a family while leaving others behind? How could this be? What about free will? Where was God in all this?

My questions went unanswered. I knew all I needed to know for the time being.

The light readings continued until lunch. I loved it, really. There was something about seeing a person's spirit in their eyes. It was humbling. Turns out that the first man I'd met that morning had the highest light reading of everyone I encountered.

The next day, it started all over again. I never was allowed to read my own daughters or my soon-to-be ex-husband. That was good. It was interesting how it worked.

I would look into someone's eyes, and I didn't really even have to give it any thought. It was just there; I would "see" their light, and the words "You will stay" or "You will be leaving" would be heard in my mind.

When I would reflect on the experience or when I told Vicky about it, I would get it mixed up, thinking that leaving would be the better option, so I would think the higher readings should be going and the lower light readings should be staying.

I had recalled the incident with them when they'd shown me the earth on fire. I'd never ever forgotten that chilling vision, so I really thought that it didn't make sense that those of a higher vibration should be the ones to experience the terrifying things I'd seen. It seemed logical to me that the higher light readings would belong to those who would be allowed to leave in order to not experience that trauma. Years later, I gained a clearer understanding of how this all might work, but at the time it concerned me greatly.

While I loved the experience of reading people's vibrations, I was torn to pieces by the information that accompanied that lesson. I kept trying to figure out how this was all going to work. It sounded too much like a science fiction movie, and I was deeply concerned for my children and for the planet as a whole.

God Beliefs

At the time, I didn't have a clear fix on God. That is, I hadn't really come to any conclusion as to what I believed, and I was regretting that very much now. My beliefs had been a work in progress, but now I needed something solid to rest on, but I found nothing. At least nothing that addressed all the unanswered questions I had in regard to all I was learning at this time. I'd left the church at the age of fifteen, which was the soonest my parents would release me from that commitment. The religious teachings didn't sit well with me—all that talk of guilt and sin.

I remember being no more than six or seven years old when I was sitting in the pew with my Sunday school teacher. We were rehearsing for the Christmas program. It was such an exciting time to be a child. The church smelled like pine trees, a sure indication of all the good things to come. I loved looking up at the big picture of Jesus with the children along with the lamb and the lion. I would gaze at it every time my parents forced us to sit through a church service. I loved Jesus and felt as if I knew him.

This day I couldn't see it from where I was sitting—the big Christmas tree was blocking my view. I looked around the sanctuary and studied the stained glass. One by one, I started to look at the other pictures I could see from this new angle when another picture behind the organ caught my eye. I'd never noticed that one before. It was another picture of Jesus, but he appeared to be in pain, and I was concerned about that. My beloved Jesus was bleeding and suffering. Why in the world would a church have a picture of such a thing? It was violent and freakish to me, as well as disgusting—it was like they were glorifying his pain. I was distraught.

I asked my Sunday school teacher what was happening to him.

"He was put up on the cross and died," she responded.

I was horrified. "Why? Who did this, and why is there a picture of it?"

She hushed me, but I persisted.

Finally she leaned down and whispered, "He died so you can have eternal life."

"What?" I was appalled, and I pulled on her sleeve.

"Why?" I asked in despair.

"Because we are born sinful, and he had to die to save us. Jesus died to save you from your sins," she said.

Now I might have been a very young child, but I knew a load of bunk when I heard it. And that was simply not true. Later when I was in about 5th grade, I learned the word "propaganda." I realized that was exactly the right word for the nonsense my Sunday school teacher had told me.

Incident with Brother

Everything that had been happening eventually got to me. Trying to make sense of the number sequence incidents and then the whole idea around the information they gave me in regard to the light reading lessons was too much. The breakdown of my marriage, my fear for my children, the loss of my normal life, and their continued harassment pushed me over the edge. I had promised myself I wouldn't burden anyone with what I was going through, but I broke that promise.

It was another Friday night, and I had to talk to someone. I was terribly frightened. I knew they were coming, and I was running like a crazed person. My girls were at friend's houses, and I was alone. I just got in my car about 9:00 that night and started to drive. I didn't know where I was going. I started to go to my parent's house but instinctively knew that would not be good. I would find no comfort there.

I tore around town like a crazy woman, not knowing where to go or what to do. I searched my mind for someone or someplace to go that might be safe. In my madness, I drove by my younger brother's house. I circled it a few times. We weren't all that close; I really only saw him at holidays, but I was desperate. I pulled into his driveway and rang his doorbell.

He was still up, but his wife had gone to bed. I started to talk—ramble, really. I doubt I made much sense. I told him of my fear and asked if I could stay there for the night. Would he do his best to keep them away from me?

"Don't let them get me, please?" I cried.

I knew that he was aware of the things I'd been experiencing, but we'd never talked about it. I was pretty certain that his attitude would most likely fall in line with the stand my parents had taken—that I was imagining or inflating some minor incidents way out of proportion. But this night I didn't care if he believed me or not; I was feeling so alone, so afraid, and so desperate. He felt like my only chance for safety.

My brother put his arms around me and told me it was okay. I was safe. This was exactly what I wanted to hear, and I went to pieces when I heard those words. My whole insides melted as the fear started to dissipate. I wasn't alone. I had a protector. I knew he really couldn't keep them away, but at least I wouldn't face them on my own this night. It was such a relief.

I was sobbing into his shirt, getting it wet with my tears, when I heard him say some words that didn't make any sense. I held my breath.

What was he saying?

I pulled back in order to hear more clearly.

This wasn't happening—please, God, this isn't happening. Why was he was berating me?

The words were ugly, saying that I'd always thought I was better than everyone else.

"Special, that's what you think you are! Huh! Well, you're not! Who do you think you are? And your daughters, too. All of you going around with your noses in the air."

I froze. I begged him to stop—it was so surreal that he would turn on me like this. I wanted to go back to how it had been just a minute before, but he was unrelenting. It was as if a tap had opened up in him, and he couldn't stop himself even if he wanted to. Years of pent up anger came out of him, and I was the target.

Frantically, I ran from the room, up the stairs, and out the door as he followed me with his tirade. His words felt like blows to my body as I scrambled into my car.

He stood in the doorway continuing his assault, "You can run, but you can't hide!" he yelled while shaking his fist at me.

My tires squealed as I tore out of his driveway with my heart pounding so hard I thought it would burst.

I decided to kill myself. I really didn't feel I had a choice. I headed out of town to find a nice big tree that I could aim my car for and drive toward it at a hundred miles per hour. It was a good plan. I drove down the stretch of road in search of my tree. I was relieved. The pain and confusion were going to be gone soon. I'd always known suicide was not a good option for anyone, but I truly was out of my mind with fear. I don't remember a whole lot of what happened next. I do remember speeding out of town, but things get fuzzy after that.

I remember a faint image of my daughters coming into the haze that was my mind, but I did believe they would be better off without me. I felt it was me that was bringing these horrific experiences to our doorstep, and I knew I was about to do the best thing for all concerned. I was determined.

Obviously, my life didn't end that night. How I got home, I do not know, but somehow I ended up back there because I woke up the next morning in my bed with only the terrible memories of the night before. I actually went down to see if my car was parked in the garage. I couldn't remember driving to my house, and a part of me wondered if I hadn't crashed the car and been brought home in an unconscious state and put to bed. A ridiculous idea, of course, but it was the only logical explanation I could come up with. So here was yet another thing to put into the box of confusion that seemed to be the basic structure of my life.

I struggled for some time with my brother's treatment of me that night. More than anything, I was bewildered by it. Eventually, I came to understand that he had his own demons and that I could no more hold a grudge against him than I could cut off my own arm. My brother was a big guy with an even bigger heart. I always felt life was hard for him. He used alcohol to anesthetize himself against the harshness he felt. Like me, it seemed he never quite fit into this world.

My Brother, the Greeter

He passed away quite suddenly in 2009. Before his transition, I visited him in hospice and asked him who he thought he was, going so soon.

"Who says you get to leave first?" I asked.

He replied that he had work to do—a job on the other side. I should not have been surprised by his answer, but I was. I asked him what the job was.

"Greeter," he answered.

That made his daughter and me chuckle.

"Greeter, like at Walmart?" we asked.

"Yup, there's going to be a lot of people leaving the planet soon, and they will need help with processing them all. That will be my job. I need to go train and get ready."

Somehow I couldn't doubt his words.

Hanging on by a Very Tiny Thread

Soon after the incident with my brother, I called Vicky and asked her to meet me for breakfast. I'm pretty sure she never realized how close I was to the edge. She laughed nervously when I told her that I was certain I was insane. I asked her, since she was a nurse, about how one goes about getting committed. I wanted her to take me to Mendota, a local mental health hospital.

I said, "I belong in a padded room. I truly do. Somebody needs to put me in a padded room."

I know she thought I was joking, and yet she must have seen glimpses of how far I'd been pushed. I told her about the sequential time incidents, about the light reading stuff, about the continual stream of new memories coming to the surface, *plus* the visits that were happening so frequently.

It was more than I could endure. I could hear myself not making any sense, just jumping from one thing to the next. Bless her heart. She tried to comfort me, but what words could she offer in such a situation?

I was asking too much. I tried to calm down and have a normal conversation as we finished our breakfast. We got up to leave, and as we were walking toward the door, I started to panic again. I hadn't resolved anything! I couldn't let her get away without a promise from her that she'd help me get committed. As we went through the airlock that went out of the building, I stopped and turned on her. I blocked her way out and once again demanded that she help me. I was determined to not let her leave without a resolution.

I saw pure fear in her eyes. I was sure she wasn't afraid *of* me, but *for* me. That hit me hard. I didn't want anyone looking at me like that; the only thing worse would be pity. So I tried to make a joke of it and walked out the door, but when I reached my car, I couldn't move. I had just played the last card I had, and I'd lost the match.

I was a wreck. Truly, I had been broken into little pieces. I searched my mind frantically for someone to turn to—a doctor, a minister, a counselor, a friend or relative. *Someone.* **Anyone.** I realized how crazy my stories were, and I knew I couldn't expect Vicky to carry the burden of seeing me through this experience—it just wasn't fair to her.

My sister had long since stopped talking to me about my encounters—not because she had abandoned me but because she was dealing with her own stressful issues of chronic depression. I simply could not burden her with my stuff, too.

Sweet Marion's Loving Support

Before too long, Marion with her sweet and gentle nature became my sounding board, the place I turned to for comfort. She was the one who listened patiently to me over and over again, as I recounted what was happening in my life. She not only let me rant and rave and carry on—all the while offering love and support—but she encouraged me to talk. She asked questions and was genuine in her interest and concern for me. I loved her like a mother.

She held meetings from time to time at her house for CUFOS, and people interested in the latest news would attend, as well as those who'd had an experience. Usually it was just a sighting of a craft of some sort, but I observed how very distressing that could be for some people. They had a need to talk about it over and over again, trying to make sense of it, trying to find a rational explanation. Marion was endlessly patient with them as she hung on every word and empathized with them.

She always said, "I just want answers. I just want to know what this is all about. Why are they here? What are they up to? I just want to know before I die."

The last time I saw Marion, she still hadn't gotten her answers, and she was still just as curious as ever. I miss her very much.

Vicky and Group UFO Sightings

Almost immediately after my breakfast with Vicky, I heard from Da. I was at home, sitting on the steps that led to my bedroom. I'd just gotten off a phone call and reached around to hang up the phone but stayed where I was sitting on the third step.

I'd dropped my head into my hands and was resting when I heard him say, "What can we do to comfort you?"

My head shot up. I'd heard his voice, but it was not audible; it was inside my head. This was not new, but it was different than the disembodied voice I'd been hearing of late. It's somewhat hard to describe. It's like a thought you have, only it's more like a voice that is inside your head, but it's a voice you recognize as not your own. And in this case, it was definitely Da.

This form of communication was less scary for me, and now I calmly responded to him by saying that I felt all alone. "Could they just stop all this and leave me alone to have a normal life?"

"No, that was not possible. There was too much invested."

I sat rubbing my head.

Da continued, "What would help you to not feel so alone?"

I gave his question serious consideration because I knew this was huge. This was my chance to have them meet my needs. It was somewhat of a victory, albeit small, but nonetheless a concession on their part in return for all they had taken from me.

After some thought, I asked if they could show themselves to my meditation group. There were about twelve people in the group, and they'd all been so supportive of me.

"Could they all have a sighting?"

"Yes," Da promised. "It will be done."

"And Vicky," I said. "Vicky needs to see something, too. Promise me Vicky will have a sighting."

"It will be done," he replied. And with that he was gone.

I didn't say a word about my deal with Da to anyone. Besides, it's not like I didn't know how crazy it all was. I never knew what to make of those conversations. Like everything else going on, I had trouble believing the conversation or his promise was real.

Well, over the course of the next few weeks, everyone in the group, except one, had a sighting of some sort. They all had different stories to share, and I was impressed to say the least. One saw a cigar-shaped ship, another a black triangular ship, another the classic silver ship, and still another saw dancing lights in the evening sky.

I don't believe I ever did say a word about the offer Da had made me, but I felt such a lift from within me, like a weight being pulled out of my stomach. This was a major turning point for me. My abductors had offered me comfort. They had reached out to me and done what they could to help alleviate some of my pain and feelings of isolation. By having my group share in the sightings of their crafts, it felt as if the burden I'd felt from these experiences had been lightened.

A Shift in Perspective

Another shift occurred in my perspective, and I moved closer to peace. I still didn't understand what it was all about, and I couldn't stop it, but I no longer felt so alone. That was huge. It was a new beginning for me.

To have support come from the very beings who were seemingly tormenting me was a major shift in my relationship with them. It was no longer about power and control, victim and tormenter. There was something more going on, and I knew I needed to look at it without fear. This act of kindness and concern on their part put everything into a new and different arena. I started to look at my encounters with them through a lens that didn't have as much fear. As soon as I did that, it all shifted. What an amazing discovery!

Perspective is everything. And I realized that a person always in every situation has the option of choosing the perspective from which an event or interaction can be observed. Suddenly, all my encounters looked different. To not feel like a victim after having been in that role for so long was liberating. That's not to say that it all became blissfully sweet with rainbows and hearts. No, that's not at all the way it went, but it was a major leap forward in my ability to see the situation more clearly.

As I applied that principle to my life, I still to this day recognize that any event or interaction with another has any number of ways a person can choose to view it. We each have our perspective, but it is based on our emotions at the time, our past experiences, and a thousand other things, including the kind of day we're having. AND, here's the thing that gets us all in trouble—the other person in the exchange has a perspective, based on that person's own set of criteria.

So was I a victim? This had been a major issue for me right from the start. It was this event that did the most to unravel that belief. And with that came freedom—the freedom to actually start to learn from these encounters and be a cooperative participant rather than identifying with the role of victim.

Now I'm going to share with you one of my most favorite stories from this whole chapter of my life. I don't know why I find it so, well, endearing, but I do. It was two or three days after the group had met, and I was in my kitchen around 6:00 p.m., emptying the dishwasher. I was bent over getting a few plates out of the bottom rack when I felt the presence of Da. That is, I felt the communication channel open up. It feels like a pipeline extends out of the top of my head and up into space. Someone had just opened up that pipeline, and as I stood up, I wasn't surprised at all to hear Da's voice.

"It is good?" came the question.

I knew what he meant. He was referring to the sightings my group had been given.

"Yes," I gushed. "Thank you so much! Thank you!"

"It is better?" he asked.

"Much better, yes. Thank you for that."

Then I asked, "Why couldn't Garth see a ship? Why didn't he get a sighting?"

I knew he really would want to have a sighting, but he was the only one who didn't report seeing anything. In answer to my query, I was given a vision of Garth—just his head and in front of his open eyes were four or five tiny little spaceships—they were, literally, inches from his eyes.

And then Da's voice, "Some are not ready."

I actually had to laugh at this. It was so clearly explained to me by the use of that vision—such a typical Grey thing to do! Then I remembered, I hadn't heard anything from Vicky, and I knew that if she'd had *any* sighting of a UFO, I'd have been the first one she would call.

Before he could go, I quickly said, "Wait! What about Vicky? Vicky didn't get her sighting."

Da's voice came back clear and strong, "It is done."

I guess I was mocking him as I said, "It is not done. She didn't have a sighting, or I would have heard."

"It is done," came the stern response.

"Hold on. Wait right there."

And with that, I walked over to the phone and dialed Vicky's number. She answered after a few rings, and the second I heard her voice I could tell she was sick with a bad cold. I had decided that I was not going to ask her straight out if she'd had a UFO sighting, but it turned out I didn't have the chance anyway. As soon as she heard it was me, she started to talk very fast. She explained she was sick—that much was obvious—and she went on to say that she'd have called me sooner because something exciting had happened.

Last weekend when she and her husband were driving into Madison, she'd seen a UFO. Even though she was sick, she exhibited a fair amount of enthusiasm about the sighting, and she told me all the details.

I felt slightly contrite as I hung up the phone. I knew Da had heard the whole thing.

Again he said, "It is done."

"Yes," I replied. "It is done. She had her sighting. Thank you. Thank you very much."

"It is good?" he asked.

"Yes, it is good." I responded.

And with that, the pipeline closed.

The key to growth is the introduction of higher dimensions of consciousness into our awareness.

Lao Tzu

Chapter 10:
Lessons from the 7th Dimension

At some point in early 1989 my abduction experiences tapered off and then stopped altogether. From start to finish this round of activity had lasted anywhere from 18-24 months with extremely intense visits occurring during the summer and fall of 1988. It was unusually brutal because I was so aware of the interaction. Generally, when these abduction experiences occur, all you're left with is missing time—if you are even aware of that.

Most times abductees do not even know they've had an encounter, but sometimes there is a sense that something is amiss, something feels off, and you might even have a partial memory of a strange incident that doesn't make sense. Many times there is a flash of a light, a loud cracking noise like the air is being split open, or a whirling type sound that feels more like vibration than sound. Other times you just feel something static in the air—that sixth sense that something is about to occur or has just occurred.

But these guys have an amazing ability to block you—that is, to cover or bury all memories of what you just experienced. There is something called a "screen memory" that they are able to induce, and it works like this:

> You're driving home from an afternoon of shopping and running errands. It's sunset and you are planning to be home in time to prepare dinner and have it on the table by 6:00. Suddenly, you see a big deer standing by the side of the road. Its eyes are huge and penetrating—you can't seem to look away. You stare into that deer's eyes as you drive by and think how strange it is to have it just stand by

the side of the road not moving and looking at you like that. You make a mental note to tell your spouse.

Next thing you know you are a half mile or so down the road, and it's one hour later than you realized. Maybe it's gotten entirely dark out. You replay your movements for the past few hours, and you go over all the details—where you were, how long you stayed at each stop, etc.—and try to figure out where you could have lost that hour. It's somewhat disturbing to you because you just can't figure out how you could so easily have lost track of time. You continue to drive along and you remember the deer, but now you're not so sure. Was it a deer or a dog? For some reason, all you seem to recall are the eyes. Maybe it was a raccoon?

By the time you pull into your garage, you've forgotten all about the lost hour and the only memory that remains of the drive home is the haunting image of the animal's eyes. You walk in the door, look at the clock, and are amazed that it's 7:00. You question it, you wonder about it, and then it quickly fades from your thoughts. And that's how they do it. You've been abducted, but there's no memory. The deer by the side of the road was a screen—a suggestion or image planted into your mind to cover the reality of what was really there—an alien, a Grey with large penetrating eyes.

Activity Appears to Stop—Early 1989

After my encounters ended in early 1989, I felt relief—but also an odd sense of sadness. Could it be that I missed them? Is this the way kidnap victims miss their abductors or a prisoner misses his jailer? There were actually a few times when I "sent" out a message to them. I was surprised to get a hazy response, not near the same as hearing Da's voice, but a response, nonetheless, saying that they were around but not in my vicinity.

It was a feeling like I was off the agenda, and it wasn't their time to be working with me. I hate admitting this, but I did walk around with a visceral sense of abandonment. I really struggled with that emotion and couldn't reconcile it within myself. I had prayed and cried and begged them to leave me alone, and now it had happened. How was it that I was missing them? I wondered if it was the sense of being watched over—taken care of—that I missed, or was it the time I spent with them? I had learned that being in that higher vibration was a bit of a kick. It came with benefits.

Four Leaf Clover Incident

As I look back over the years, I can see a pattern of the influences that higher frequency brings with it. There was that day toward the end of our marriage when Tom went with me to help put up a real estate sign. We'd been experiencing a fair amount of animosity as we moved through the divorce process, and I think we were both grateful to have a respite from the anger that had been brewing. We were out in a field that was almost waist-high with clover. After the sign was in the ground, we started to walk back toward the car. It was a gorgeous day out, so we lingered a bit, as neither of us was anxious to go back to work.

I had been looking up at the sky and making my way slowly to the car when I turned to see what Tom was doing. He was bent over, his face just inches from the clover as he gently ran his hands along the top. He reminded me so much of a little boy at that moment, and I was overcome with love. I watched him for a few seconds more before I asked him what he was doing.

"Looking for a four-leaf clover," he responded.

The love that I'd been feeling swelled up within me, and I saw him as he truly is—pure and innocent. This was unconditional love. It filled my being and I knew I had been given a gift.

I looked at him and he held my gaze as I said, "Here, I will get one for you."

I reached out my hand and without looking away from his eyes, I closed my fingers around the stem of a clover. I knew it didn't matter which one I chose. I felt a charge not unlike a current of electrical energy move through my fingers and into the plant. I squeezed the stem for a moment before I plucked the clover and held it out to him. I never looked at it.

I said, "Here, take this and put it somewhere safe—someplace where you can take it out and look at it when life gets hard, and it will get hard. You have challenges ahead of you, but remember this moment and know that miracles happen. Know without doubt that you are loved. You are always loved, and you are *never* alone."

He accepted the four-leaf clover, and as he stared at it, he asked me how I did that, but I couldn't answer. There were other moments similar to that one throughout my time with the Greys. These kinds of experiences that seem so miraculous to us here in this dimension are not considered anything special in the higher frequencies. Life flows more easily when you are closer to your Source, and that is where you are when you go up that ladder into the higher dimensions. Miracles such as this are available to us all if we can exist in a state of pure love, for that is the highest vibration there is—unconditional love.

Missing My Guys

While I didn't have a lot of memory about what actually occurred during those many hours I'd spend in their company, I did have recall of the lessons they'd taught me and the overall sense that it had all been to serve a higher purpose. Now I was missing them, and my life seemed to pale. Was this a clue to unraveling the mystery? I am not beyond looking at what part this could play in having brought about this interaction.

Was I creating these experiences in an effort to make myself feel more important?

I followed that trail of thought deep within myself and looked at it as objectively as I could. It had been determined that the experiences I was having were physically real. That is, they determined that it was not happening in my imagination or dreams. I had certainly wished for that to be the case as that would have been something I could have made sense of.

But this, the idea that aliens were coming and taking me for one or two-hour increments in order to prepare me to play some role in the future drama that was about to unfold in humanity's development—well, that wasn't something I could have ever made up. First of all, I would have had to have knowledge of alien abductions in order to dream this up, and I was so innocent of anything having to do with ufology. To be honest, if I was going to have fantasies of grandeur, this would not have been the way I would have gone!

This does not bring any kind of wanted attention with it but instead brings ridicule and labels I'd rather not be identified with, such as crazy or delusional. At the time all this came to the surface, I was a serious-minded young woman conducting business that required I be trustworthy and competent. The last thing I would have gone looking for was a story that brought a high level of weirdness with it—one that would easily result in shame for me and my family. These are the thoughts I struggled with back in the summer of 1989 as I tried to let go of the whole nightmare I'd been living.

Moving Forward

I eventually picked up the pieces of my life and did my best to move forward with a normal life. There it was again—that wish to have a normal life. But what is normal? I certainly no longer knew. My compass was broken, and I would never again be the same, but that didn't stop me from trying as I buried myself in my work and did my best to let it all go. But I was not able to forget what I'd been through.

It was always there, always in the background, and sometimes it would come abruptly to the surface when something would trigger a memory or a sense of knowingness would come into my awareness. Over the years, my abduction memories continued to fill in, little by little. I was remembering details of the actual abductions, but more and more what I was recalling were the things they had taught me, starting when I was a child. It was like the layers of an onion were being peeled away. I was no longer as interested in the details, the nuts and bolts, of what had happened to me. That seemed secondary.

Instead, it felt like I was coming awake, and the more awake I became, the more aware I was of how ridiculous it all was. Life, that is. There was something missing—something huge that most of us seemed to be missing. I needed to find out what it was.

The little meditation group that had played such a huge role in keeping me sane disbanded, and for the next seventeen years I followed my own inner guide as I went looking for answers. Mostly, though, I did my best to live a regular life. I needed the respite.

There was college tuition to pay, weddings to plan for my daughters, and a new life as a single woman to experience. During this time, I would have moments when I would seem to become aware of a lesson or an idea that clearly seemed to stem from my time with them. It would be a way of perceiving life that I could not link to anything else I'd read or studied.

I'd forgotten about the words the healer had told me. I wouldn't have even remembered them had I not made note of them in a diary that I found while writing this book. His analogy of the capsule dissolving was a good one because that is exactly what it seems to be. For about seventeen years, I lived a pretty normal life in spite of it all. But then things began to change—very quickly.

It is apparent to me that everything in my life has been planned. There is a schedule, and I am going along with the agenda, no longer struggling and fighting against the course my life is on. It is clear to me that I agreed to be a participant in this odyssey, and I am now happy to oblige. And just as clearly as if I'd received a telegram, I knew that it was time to write a book and tell the story of my alien encounters, but the most important part of the story would not be about the fear and trauma I experienced in coming to terms with all this or the dialogue about what they did to me. No. The most significant part of the book is The Three Important Things to Know.

Three Important Things to Know

#1. We Are One with Our Creator.

As this capsule dissolved in my mind, I began to clearly remember being taught these three crucial lessons. They had spent a lot of time making sure I understood each and every one. The most critical thing they wanted me to know, and they started teaching it to me at a very young age, no more than five, was this: **We are all One with our Creator**.

This lesson has now become a fairly well-known hypothesis, but back in the mid-1950s it was a pretty radical idea. I remember the Greys driving this point home for me over and over again. I didn't get it. How could I be part of God and part of every living thing? But it finally started to take hold when they gave me a visual demonstration around the age of eight.

A man was sitting at a kitchen table. It might have been my father. I was positioned behind him and above, looking down over his shoulders, so I never saw his face. His large hands were out in front of him, resting on the red and white checked table cloth, and there were dining utensils sitting near his right hand. Suddenly, he picked up the fork with his right hand and stabbed it deeply into his left hand. It was shocking and very jarring for me to witness. It upset me very much.

Calmly, Da stated, "This is what you do when you harm another person. You may as well do to yourself the very thing you think you are doing to another because that is exactly what you are doing. You *are* doing it to yourself because there is no difference between you and any other living thing. We are all One."

This lesson was expanded on almost every time I was with them. They took the idea deeper and deeper until it became a core belief for me.

They talked about how this one simple lesson was all humanity really needed to get in order to change the world. Just this one thing—known and really understood by all humans—would change the path of destruction we were on.

"How could we not know this?"

At times I could feel their frustration with us. We are all One with our Creator. It was vitally important to learn. As time passes, this lesson becomes more and more meaningful to me. I had always felt a connection with nature and held a deep reverence and love for this earth. As a child, I felt especially protective toward trees and believed that I could feel their energy and even communicate with them.

To this day, I feel that bond, but I never felt much connection to humans. I always felt as if God had made a mistake by putting me here. I didn't fit in. In general, I will admit that I never understood the human being very much; overall, they appeared to be rather selfish and ruthless. My feelings toward humanity eventually shifted and changed as I came into awareness, but in my younger years I struggled a lot with being classified as a human.

Over the years and throughout the course of many, many encounters, the Greys showed me in so many ways how **we are one with all living things—*all living things*. Not just nature, not just the pretty things, not just people we like, but *all* living things, all sentient beings, everywhere throughout the Universe.** This concept needs to become more than just an idea, more than just a bumper sticker. It needs to become integrated into our very Being. And how is this supposed to happen?

Through awareness. By awakening from the unconscious state in which most of us stumble through life. Stop for a minute and look at how we live our lives. We are racing through life with our heads down—everyone in a hurry all day long, day after day, living our lives for the next moment, the next big thing.

Fear is the motivating factor—fear that we won't *have* enough, that we won't *be* enough, that we won't *be worthy* enough. We're so distracted that we never take the time to inquire as to who or what is at the core of our very nature.

We need to question our place in the cosmos. Our attention is on *things*. Do you see how silly that is? We have forgotten who we are. We have lost our connection to Source. We need to find that lost connection. We need to remember who we are and what we were created to be. Somehow it got lost in all the drama of life.

Do you ever wonder why that is? Do you ever wonder why life appears to be so complicated and confusing? Do you ever question if this is the life our Creator had planned for us— one of pain, fear, and death? The answers are here, but you need to have the passion and desire to truly want to know. It is the most amazing journey you can take.

It was easier for me to accept that I was one with all things, but it took me longer to accept that we are One with God. As a matter of fact, I didn't really get it. I mean *really* get it until recently. Like so many, I'd been taught the childhood lesson that God was a man who sat on a throne and ruled over the world. He became angry with us when we did something bad, and He judged us and punished us for those bad things. I was taught to fear God—all while they told me to love Him and pray to Him. God was just one step above Santa Claus, but in truth Santa was easier to believe in, relate to—and, yes, to love.

How did the world manage to get this all turned upside down and backwards? How could the very institutions that were put in place to teach us about unconditional love, end up teaching us guilt and such a distorted brand of love that humanity as a whole became dysfunctional? I remember visiting a sheep farm in Ireland. To get the sheep to go anywhere, it was best to get one headed off in the right direction because all the rest would just follow—even to the point of following the lead sheep off a cliff. They just all blindly followed. That appears to be what most of us do.

We are taught that God is separate from us, but the truth is completely the opposite. We are extensions of our Creator and our very essence is shared with Him. We are to God as a drop is to the ocean. The ocean is not quite complete without that drop and certainly cannot exist as the ocean without the many drops. *The Course in Miracles* states "Without you there would be a lack in God, a Heaven incomplete, a son without a Father." (T-pg. 511) We have forgotten our very essence. It is our belief in the separation that has kept humanity in bonds, and until we can see God in every person we meet, we are destined to remain in this fear-dominated world.

We are all one with our Creator. As I see it, this concept ties into the Greys' whole purpose. We, as humans, need to wake up to this idea and really *get* it. We need to understand just how wrong it is to have children dying of starvation, how wrong it is to have our brothers sleeping on the sidewalks at night, how terribly wrong it is to have anyone go without medical care just because that person doesn't have a lot of money. Are we crazy?

Yes. We are a race of beings that has gone insane. But at our core at the very essence of our being, there is light. And it simply is not possible for that light to go out entirely. It can be forgotten. It can become very dim or hidden, but it cannot be extinguished. And thank God for that—literally.

There's a lot of bad press out there about my guys, the Greys. Among most ufologists, the general consensus is that they are evil and have a selfish agenda. On the surface, this can certainly appear to be true. Perhaps I have a different perspective because I had to come up with an acceptable belief in order to survive the trauma of my experiences, but I find it extremely difficult to believe them evil when I look at all they taught me.

I think they are from the 7th dimension. I cannot say that like a lot of my memories, I have clear recall of them giving me that information. Instead, it seems to be something that I just know. When I recently asked Da if he was a Zeta (grey), his response surprised me. He said that making that statement about him would not be an accurate accounting of who he is.

When I said, "Then tell me who you are and where you come from," he responded that he is a "Voyager of the Universe, going where needed in service to the Creator."

I said, "Well, you look like a Zeta. Why is that?"

And again his response was surprising. He explained that his body is more etheric and that he dons that container when coming into this dense environment. He went on to say that many visitors to planet earth use the Zeta type body because it is highly functional in this vibration. So with that statement I believe he confirmed another belief I held but never knew how I knew—that the big, black eyes they all have are not really their eyes but some sort of goggle or shade. Not because our sun is so bright, but because *their* light is so brilliant.

If you recall the light reading lessons where they taught me that we all have an inner light based on the level of our vibration, I would have to say that they have an extremely high vibration or light reading compared to ours. We can easily see the level of light in people's eyes, and so it would seem that an extraordinarily high vibration or light might be more than we could tolerate.

It is always so wonderful to look into Da's eyes and experience the acceptance and love I see there. I know that is contrary to most reports concerning the Greys, but would he be considered a Grey in view of what I just learned? Regardless, there is no doubt that there is a high level of strangeness to the interaction you experience with ETs. Anyone who has had these encounters will confirm that. Unfortunately, most people report that it was not a pleasant experience, but again, I will remind you of the fear factor. Any experience we have becomes distorted when it is filtered through high emotion and particularly when that emotion is fear.

Oddly enough or so it seemed to me for years was their idea of what they considered to be the second most important thing to know. This one was a mouthful, and like the others, it was drummed into me until it was like a mantra. The real meaning of it escaped me for such a long time that I'm sure I must have frustrated them to no end.

#2. We Are Multi-dimensional Beings on Multiple Levels.

"We are multi-dimensional beings existing on more than one level at a time" was the statement I was expected to not just repeat upon demand but also understand. Again, this lesson started when I was very little, and I had absolutely no idea what they were trying to convey to me. It started to fall into place with one of the visual lessons they gave me, one of many, but this one finally jump-started my comprehension.

They showed me a stack of thin papers like we used back in the old days. I believe it was called "onion paper" because it resembled the skin of an onion. There were a lot of them loosely stacked on top of one another, and they reached a height of 10-12 inches.

"Each of those pieces of paper represents a life," they told me.

Then they took a long pencil-type object that was sharpened on the end and stabbed it down through the center of the stack.

"This is you," they said.

Okay. I started to understand. Given the other lessons they'd been teaching me, I understood that the pencil was my essence, my life force. It was explained that the aspect that was me was able to be present in these many different levels even though they were happening at the same time.

I came to understand that our essence vibrates at different rates, depending on where in this beam of light you put your attention—the higher you go, the faster and more pure the vibration—so the experiences are in different dimensions and different timelines. Accordingly, each of the lives being experienced at the same time can and does influence what is happening in the other dimensions.

As you know, they do not experience time in the same manner we do in the three dimensional world, and they were always diligent about pointing that out to me—which is part of the reason this lesson was so difficult for me to grasp. Eventually when I started to understand this concept, they changed the wording to "We are multi-dimensional beings existing on more than one level *simultaneously*."

I didn't particularly like this lesson, and I certainly didn't embrace it the way I eventually did the first lesson. It was complicated for me as a child, and as an adult I didn't understand why it was so important to know.

Now I get it. And I hope I can make it clear to you as well, for it really is a significant clue as to who we are. It actually ties into the first lesson, which is essentially the lesson of Oneness. This just expands on that premise and puts it into terms we should be able to understand.

I had an experience when I was a young mother of about twenty-six that helped me relate to one element of this lesson. I was home alone with my two young daughters, and it was about 9:00 at night. Both girls were asleep, and their dad was working and not due home for a couple more hours. I was watching TV in bed when I had the strangest sensation.

I don't have the words to explain it, but I suddenly seemed to feel lost. I was terribly frightened, and I didn't understand what was going on. Instinctively, I jumped out of bed and ran into the bathroom. I looked into the mirror and "saw" a woman with a curly head full of red hair, green eyes, and a freckled, pale complexion. She wore dated clothing that I would define as "old European." She was young—I'd guess about seventeen—and stocky and solid.

Now when I say that I saw this girl, it is hard to explain, but it wasn't that I had physically turned into her, but I would put it in these terms: I was seeing with her eyes and with her memory of what *should be* there—and in a sense *was* there. I was also still here, but it was like she was transposed over me. I leaned in close to the mirror and looked into my/her eyes, trying to understand what was happening.

165

I could "hear" the girl's thoughts in my head; they were separate from my own confused thoughts, and they were of such a strong brogue that it startled me. I knew who I was, but that expression of me was sharing this space with another being. I understood I was seeing another aspect of myself. This young lady was me but in another dimension. This event happened before my abduction experiences came to the surface, and yet I understood. My fear was replaced with understanding and a sense of knowing. I actually felt a kind of kinship with this girl and was about to ask some questions of her when just as quickly as it had occurred, the young lass was gone.

That was a radical way to learn the multi-dimensional lesson, and it was very basic. The meaning of this lesson goes much deeper than just knowing that we are experiencing different lives at what we would consider to be the same time. This lesson is more about vibration. If in another dimension there is great trauma or a giant step forward in awareness or any other really momentous happening that affects the growth and awakening of the spirit in that dimension, it is felt in the other dimensions.

Think about it. It has to be that way. Since the core essence connects you to the other dimensions, you cannot *not* be impacted on all levels by what is occurring on any one of the other levels. Truth be told, every little thing going on affects all the other experiences you are having, but it doesn't really have a strong impact until it resonates on a deep soul level. The pencil image of who we are is not our spirit; it is our soul, our connection to Source. The awareness that is present in each dimension is an aspect of the one self, the spirit. The higher up the pencil you go, the higher the vibrational frequency. Thus the statement, we are multi-dimensional beings.

But do you see how this connects us all? At the lower vibrational level are those expressions of our self that are operating in a denser world, and at the higher frequencies, well, that may very well be where we find our connection to the Creator. Do you see how this must end with the inevitable conclusion that you are me and I am you? We really are on some level experiencing each life that has ever occurred or ever will occur. Profound? Yes.

Now I am going to add to this confusing topic by explaining that not only are we experiencing different lives in different time frames and seemingly different bodies, but we are also having experiences in what would be considered parallel universes. That is, there are other timelines where our lives are playing out a different scenario than the one we appear to be having in the here and now.

How is this possible? Because every thought we have creates a reality. There are, literally, an infinite number of timelines or alternate realities where our lives are being experienced. We are moving quickly toward the time when these timelines will be easily accessed as we ascend into the higher frequencies.

It is our job at this particular juncture in humanity's development to bring all the aspects of our selves—all of those multi-dimensional selves—into alignment. It is time to awaken and time to bring all those many slivers of light together into a mighty beam of light and love. If you picture your core essence as a pillar of light, you would be close to the truth. But now, come in close to that ray of light and see parts of it where there is a disconnect and other places where there are little chunks of matter blocking the light and keeping it from flowing freely.

Those are the places where you are harboring grievances and carrying around pain from the mistaken belief that another has wronged you. When you realize just how impossible that is since *there is nobody else out there*—remember there is only one of us—see what that does to your feelings about being a victim. All that we believe has been done to us, we really did to ourselves. It cannot be otherwise. Now is the time to come into this awareness. Now is the time to open up that channel of light and let go of the blocks. It is time to let our light flow freely between the dimensions of our being and upward through the higher vibrations and home to Oneness—home to God.

A discussion on the multi-dimensional aspects of who we are could become extremely complicated and a final explanation will never be found that would satisfy everyone. Trying to define the truth of what and who we are cannot really be put into words, but the answer is readily available to all who sincerely seek it. There's never been a time in the development of humanity to more easily access the answers.

"We are multi-dimensional beings existing on more than one level simultaneously."

If we over-analyze the meaning, we lose sight of its simplicity. It sounds complicated, but it is not. Dimensions, like time, are fluid and ultimately just an illusion.

The spark of light that exists in each and every soul is the Divine. We are simply God experiencing Himself—the Creator playing in His Creation. We are eternal beings, and that is the truth of who we are at our core. Anything that is not eternal—anything that can die or perish—is not of our Creator. God would not give life to something that would die. The world and all the forms that exist in it, including our bodies, were not created by God. It is our thoughts manifesting as reality that we are experiencing. That is why we can exist on so many different levels and timelines. A loving Father would never create a world of pain and death, such as exists on this three-dimensional planet. The part of us that is eternal—our soul—was created by our loving Father. By remembering the true essence of who you are and realizing that your connection to Source can never be broken is where you will find deep, unshakeable peace.

My purpose in writing this book is not to try to convince you to fall in line with my beliefs but to challenge you to seek out your own answers to the questions I might be raising for you. It's not important whether you accept my explanation or not; the only thing that matters is that you feel inspired, provoked, curious, or challenged enough to search beyond the traditional teachings and begin the journey inward where the answers to who you truly are reside.

And that brings me to their final lesson—the third most important thing to know. This lesson is extremely useful, and I would humbly suggest that if you are not already practicing this, that you would consider trying it as the results are life-changing. It's a simple statement and one that is fairly popular already.

#3. Monitor Your Thoughts.

This teaching impacted my life in a way I can't even begin to describe. As with the other lessons, they took this one much deeper than it appears to be in the simple form it is offered. They started out by teaching me that everything that is happening in the world is a result of our thoughts. Every thought that every person has creates an energy stream, and it brings about the life we consider to be our reality. They were very harsh in explaining that the reason our planet is one filled with pain, trauma, war, disease, and disasters is because of one simple reason: our thoughts—our fear-based thoughts. We project these ideas out, and they are mirrored back to us in the form of seemingly physical experiences. Unfortunately, the validation created by having our fearful thoughts mirrored back to us in the form of life experiences also contributes to the downward spiral. We believe the world is an unsafe place and that we can be harmed, and so we project that. It becomes our reality and, therefore, reinforces the fearful thought and creates more fearful thoughts. No wonder our world is in such a state!

It is the collective thoughts of all humanity that are creating our reality, and because we live in a world of form, it is our tendency to try to change the world on the level of form. In other words, we try to change the world by changing the *effect* rather than the *cause*. I will use the analogy most often used in trying to explain this concept.

Think of a movie. You cannot change what is happening in the movie by going up and messing with the screen (the effect); you need to get to the projector (the cause) and make the change there. So it is with life. Our life, that is, our reality (the effect) is the movie, and the projector is our thoughts (the cause). As *A Course in Miracles* puts it, "You perceive from your mind and project your projections outward." (T-pg. 98) And so it is that we cannot bring about change in this world until we change our thoughts.

Now that concept takes us right back to the number one most important thing to know—the lesson of Oneness. It all connects together. Our thoughts do affect everyone else on the planet. We have a responsibility to ourselves and to all humanity to bring about the desired change that is needed by simply changing our thoughts. We need to realize it is counterproductive to demonstrate or protest for change when it is done in anger or fear. We are an evolving species, and we have been stuck in ego-based thoughts long enough. It is time for us to step into the light and into the awareness of who we are and claim our identity. It is time for us to understand how this world we inhabit works.

While they were teaching me the overall effects of our thoughts on the planet, they also had me apply the lesson on a more personal scale. They showed me that we create our reality on a day-by-day basis, depending on what vibration or energy we put out in the form of our thoughts. At first, it is not easy to monitor your thoughts, but it becomes second nature after diligently practicing for some time. What they told me was to be aware of the voice that seemed to speak inside my head—those thoughts are directing my life. I can change them. They are not random. I can and should replace any negative or fearful thought with ones that are positive and loving. They stressed that my life will be whatever my thoughts are, and we cannot afford to allow thoughts of fear to dominate. You change your thoughts—you change your life. It was that simple. And so it is.

They stressed to me that all illness and disease originate in your mind. And that healing does not take place by "fixing" the body but by changing your thoughts. The body is at the command of the mind—they drilled that into me, as well. Visualization is a powerful tool whether it is used to bring about a more healthy body or bring a wanted change into your life.

When I was just twenty-one years old, I was diagnosed with a form of arthritis. The doctor told me I would not be able to hike, ride a bike, or be very active as this form of arthritis would eventually incapacitate me. I remember the pain in my joints being so bad that it was interfering with my sleep, and walking was becoming an issue. One night I came awake with the knowingness that I could release this malady from my body. I remembered hearing an explanation about how our body is no different than the house you live in, and if something becomes broken, like a window, you don't continue to live in the house with the broken window. You repair it. And so it is with the body.

They told me to visualize the area where the pain was located and to "see" the pain. I did this. I envisioned the pain as a dark green almost black tar-like substance that was wrapped around my knee. I felt it in there. I saw it creating pain for me. Then I visualized it being pulled out of my body. As I did this, I could feel it come out. Once it was out, I got a little panicky, wondering what I should do with this inky, nasty stuff.

I was told to give it to the earth so it could heal and neutralize it. I didn't like that answer, but I was told that the earth was happy to do that for me. It was healing for all involved, and so I saw myself take the nasty stuff outside where I quickly found a large boulder—I just couldn't bear to put it directly into the earth. I asked the rock first if it was okay that I give this to it, and I got a positive response, so I watched this inky substance be absorbed into the boulder.

It all sounds crazy, I know, talking to a rock, but that is exactly as it occurred. The bottom line is I never had trouble with my joints again. I've used this method many times and almost always with success. I have no doubt this technique was taught to me by the Greys. And I am grateful.

The other aspect of thought-monitoring and the lesson of oneness relates to the innate need humans have to judge one another. If we really understood the lesson of oneness, then we would quickly realize how silly but damaging this practice is. The awakening that is taking place on earth right now is quickly bringing about this necessary change. As those people who have come into awareness practice acceptance of everyone and everything, they are demonstrating for us just how beautiful life can be when it is lived in a state of gratitude and forgiveness. Aligning with your Higher Self/Source/whatever name you want to give it is a simple pursuit that can bring about profound change in your life and the lives of all on this planet. Each individual has much, much more impact than is realized.

And so it is that I have deep gratitude for all I experienced and learned through these encounters. These three lessons, The Three Important Things to Know, are all we really need to understand and implement in order to realize a tremendous change for humanity—one that we are destined to experience. So in reading this book, it matters not one itty bitty tiny bit if you believe any of my story, for that was not the purpose in writing it. I have no concern if you choose to dismiss the whole thing as a dream or illusion or mental illness or anything else. The fact is, I never had any interest in telling my story until it was revealed to me that I needed to share these three truths.

I am not, by any means, the first person to put these lessons out there. Many, many others have done so and will continue to do so, and all have done it much more eloquently than I have been able to do. Still I offer to you these teachings in the hope that it creates an opening, a curiosity, a spark to look further within to find your own answers.

It's exhilarating to be alive in a time
of awakening consciousness;
it can also be confusing, disorienting, and painful.
Adrienne Rich

Chapter 11:
What Are You Doing Back Here?

A Time of Testing

When I was ten years old, the Greys told me that there would come a time when I would be tested.

"Tested?" I asked. "About what?"

I was used to them testing me about The Three Important Things to Know, as well as all the other lessons they'd been trying to convey to me, so I wasn't overly concerned about this, except there was a more serious overtone to this comment than usual.

I was sitting on the floor working on a puzzle as Da sat quietly nearby in a chair, watching me. Now I looked up and gave him my full attention. He was leaning in close and in his eyes I saw not just love, but deep concern. I got a little uncomfortable, and I instinctively felt scared.

"There will come a time when great changes will take place on your planet, and in the early stages of that event you will be tested. You will lose many things in your life, including your home and members of your family," was his somber response.

I wasn't expecting that answer, and I felt a small bubble of fear rise up in me as I asked if there was going to be a war and "Would a bomb fall on my house killing everyone except me?"

Looking back, I realize that to a ten-year-old that would be the most reasonable explanation for losing your home and family. I was too young to understand the dynamics of adult life.

He assured me there would be no bomb, but nonetheless, this crisis was going to occur. He went on to say it was necessary for certain life lessons to be experienced by me, and so this event was programmed into my life and would start to occur somewhere around the year 2009.

I didn't understand what was meant by any of it, but I never forgot it.

Apparently, it came into my conscious memory as my family rode along in our car soon after I'd been told this bit of news. I was still young—no more than eleven years old. We were on our way to my aunt's house for some function, and I remember exactly where we were outside of Madison.

I thought about what I'd been told. Again I will explain that I really didn't know *who* had given me this information, but it was there, and I knew without doubt that it was true. I thought about the year 2009. That was an odd number, and at first I couldn't comprehend how we could ever get to that year. I asked my father, who was driving the car, and he explained that when we reached 1999 the next year would be 2000 and then 2001, 2002, and so on.

Oh my goodness! That seemed an awfully long way off! This was 1961 and I couldn't even imagine living that long, so I used all my fingers and toes to figure out how old I would be when this terrible thing would happen to me and my family. It took me a few attempts, but finally I figured out I would be 59. Well, that was awfully close to 60, and that was OLD as far as I was concerned, so I was tremendously relieved.

By that time, what did it matter if I lost my family, we'd all be so old by then anyway! So I stopped stressing about it and put it away on that shelf I kept in my mind for such odd things.

I did take it down and look at it from time to time. I wondered about it. I alternated between believing it and denying the reality of it. After all, they'd taught me about the power of our thoughts, and I just refused to put any energy into that distressing idea. So I wasn't really expecting anything of any magnitude to occur, and the closer we came to the year 2009, the more I chose to doubt it until it happened seemingly with a life all its own.

"The perfect storm" is how someone described the dismantling of my life. I watched in amazement, as one thing or person after another disappeared. My business and career, many of my friends and intimate relationships, family members, money, possessions, property, and all the labels that I'd used to describe myself. It was like the lights went out one day and never came back on. All the boundaries and perimeters that had defined who I was and what my life was about were gone.

My life had become an empty canvas. The cuts had been swift and deep. I had been gutted—or had I? Thanks to what I'd learned as a result of my prior experiences with the Greys, I had a pretty strong foundation under me. It was not possible for me to play the part of victim ever again, and so as each loss occurred, I was *eventually* able to look at it and seek the higher meaning behind the experience. There was a strong sense that all was as it was meant to be and that everything was going exactly according to plan. That's not to say I didn't falter because I certainly did. I stumbled and fell more than once.

I didn't know how to slow down. I needed to learn how to relax, to stop trying to fix everything and put all that was breaking in my life back together again. When the recession first hit in the fall of 2007, I continued to go into my office in spite of the fact that there simply was no work. Eventually, it dawned on me that with winter on its way, it didn't make any sense for me to stay in Wisconsin, so one day I packed up my car, grabbed my little Maltese, and left for Texas.

My intention was to try to visit my daughter whom I was estranged from and my grandson for a while before heading over to Arizona for the duration of the winter. I arrived in Austin only to be turned away by my daughter, so I left without seeing her or my grandson.

My heart was heavy as I headed west across the plains of Texas. I went as far as I could before stopping at a trucker's motel along the way. Then I set out again early the next morning. I was less than two hours out of Tucson on Hwy 10. Traffic was heavy—too heavy for the two lanes we were traveling on.

My little seven-pound dog and I traveled well together. It was a bit of a chore sneaking him into the hotels at night, but it was worth it to have him with me. We had a good routine. He'd ride for a while on my lap, then get up and go into his bed that was positioned in the back of my SUV. Food and water were available to him, and we could drive for six hours straight without having to stop. He was good company.

The speed limit through the desert was 75, and traffic that day was moving as a solid wall at about 82 mph. My sweet Pookie was curled up on my lap, sleeping innocently. I was trying to make it to Tucson in time to have dinner with my parents who were wintering there.

Car Incident #3—2007—Impossible!

Right outside Benson there was a short on-ramp that didn't give very much room for the merging vehicles to move into the flow of the traffic already flying down the interstate. I was driving my SUV in the passing lane and was just starting to move up alongside a semi. On my right in the next lane was a white SUV—a Ford, I think. I watched as a motorcycle with a passenger on it and another car, a red SUV, came screaming down the on-ramp. I mean they were really flying.

This highway through the Arizona desert had virtually no shoulder along the left lane. We were a solid wall of vehicles, and there was no place for the motorcycle or the red SUV to go. And yet, down they came into the traffic.

I watched as the motorcycle drove up alongside the rear wheel of the semi and balanced on the thin shoulder along that side of the road. It was frightening. Time slowed down as all this happened in less than a few seconds, but my observations and thoughts seemed to go on for a minute or more. The red SUV came into traffic against the white SUV that was next to me. She had nowhere to go but to move over against me and force me off the road.

I had been watching the traffic around me and knew that I had a solid line of cars behind me in both lanes. There was room for me to move up alongside the semi, but there was no time—the white SUV was coming over. I knew that I had to make a terrible decision, but really there was no decision to make. I had to drive my car off into the median in order to avoid a larger loss of life.

I remember thinking that at least seven vehicles would be involved if I let the white SUV hit me. And what would be the purpose in that? Odds were I would die along with several others, not to mention all who would be severely injured. I decided to turn my car into the median to allow room for the white SUV, which would in turn make room for the red SUV and motorcycle. There really was no other choice as I'd tried accelerating and moving into the open space alongside the semi, but there simply was no time.

It's strange what happens to time at moments like that. I took all that in, in less than a second. And I still had time to glance down at the sleeping dog in my lap. I loved him so much, and I felt so bad, knowing that he was going to die in the next moment as the air bag would deploy and crush him. I thought of my youngest daughter and how angry she would be to lose her mother and her beloved Pookie at the same time. I thought of my oldest daughter and felt sadness. I sent immense love to both of them and prayed that my youngest would forgive me and that my oldest would not feel guilt about the way things had been between us when I died.

Yes, I was going to die. There was little doubt about that.

I was going at least 85 mph now as I'd sped up to try to get out of the way of the white SUV, and I was about to drive into a bunch of scrub trees at that speed. I certainly hoped I would die as the alternative didn't seem too appealing. All those thoughts in the blink of an eye.

I tightened my grip and gently turned the wheel—I didn't want to jerk it hard and spin out of control, so instead I kept

The Forgotten Promise

pace with the white SUV's movement toward me. I looked down the median and saw the tree I was pretty certain would be the one to mangle my car and end my life. I kept my eye on that tree and aimed for it. I waited to hear the crunch of the gravel and to feel the pull as I passed over the little strip of shoulder, but there was no change.

I stayed steady in my lane. So I turned the wheel a bit more, but still I did not move toward the median. I started to brace for the inevitable crash from the white SUV hitting my passenger door as she had been inches from me. I didn't understand what was happening, but clearly my plan wasn't working, and now the horrific crash I'd wanted to avoid was going to occur.

Only it didn't. Another miracle, unexpected and so gratefully accepted, came into my life. When I brought my eyes back to the road and off the tree in the median, which we had just passed, I saw with utter amazement that the white SUV was now in front of me, driving alongside the semi.

How the hell did that happen?

I looked at my front fender and noted that it was no more than two feet off the back wheel of that truck. Indeed, I couldn't even see the bottom of its back tire, I was that close. It was absolutely impossible for her to have somehow squeezed in between me and that semi.

Impossible.

I looked at the vehicle ahead of me, and I will never forget the woman in that SUV. She was bouncing up and down and sideways. I don't know what she experienced, but clearly she knew something had just happened that should not have happened according to the laws of this world.

Once again my angels had spared my life. Or was it the Greys? Whoever it was, I felt gratitude. I didn't want to die like that, leaving pain and unfinished business behind for my loved ones. My dog never even woke up—he just stayed curled up in my lap, totally oblivious to what had just happened.

I shared my story with a few people, but they pretty well minimized it by saying I must have misjudged the distance between my car and the semi.

No, I didn't. But I stopped talking about it.

It is just another example of how the human mind can't easily accept anything that is not within the confines of how we are taught this world should function.

But for me, it was more validation that there are dimensions and worlds within worlds. There is so much more to who we are and what our world is than what we are able to see, touch, feel, hear, or taste.

Living in the Now

I spent that winter and the next few in the desert, letting the healing energy that resides there work its magic. I learned to observe my life from a higher perspective and allow the miracles to show up on a daily basis, as I sought answers to the bigger questions of life. I eventually came to understand that my seeming losses were a clearing out of the old, so I could make way for the new. Not just a new life but a new way of looking at life.

I came to appreciate the journey I was on, and I learned to surrender my will and trust in a higher power. Surrender is an odd word. It implies weakness, but I now know it is a show of strength to trust in your higher self and live in alignment with that energy rather than trying to control life from the limited perspective we have in this three-dimensional world.

I learned to live in the "now" moment, and as I did, everything began to flow effortlessly. I gave up trying to fix my broken life. I gave up fighting with life. I did a prayer of surrender every morning. By doing so, I knew without a doubt that whatever showed up was in my highest and best interest—even if it didn't initially seem that way. Over and over again I would be witness to the miracle of living life in complete trust.

Da and Crew Re-appear—September 2010

It was September of 2010, and I was home in Wisconsin when Da and a few of his companions suddenly showed up in my bedroom one night. My composure and calmness were a pleasant surprise to me, but I won't take complete credit for it, as I'm certain they had me in an altered state. Greeting them as if it were an everyday occurrence to have aliens drop by in the middle of the night, I serenely asked them what they were doing back here. It's virtually unheard of for them to abduct or involve themselves in the lives of anyone after a certain age, and I'd passed that age some time ago.

Da seemed insulted. "We told you we'd be back when the earth changes started, and those changes are happening now. You know the training you were given. There is work to be done" was his typical, no-nonsense reply.

I actually got kind of excited and said, "So I get to do the light reading thing?"

Da, still not one to mince words, said, "It is done."

I responded, "What? You did it without me!"

"No," he said, "it was done with you. You just don't remember."

I was really bummed by that information and expressed as much to him. I wanted to know how that was possible and when it had been done. Then I stopped short as I realized the implications of what I'd just been told.

"Wait, mankind didn't make the cut?" I asked with dread—not really wanting to hear the answer.

He promptly "dropped" the information into my mind, and it was huge. Staggering.

Then because I'm sure he knew it was much more than I could comprehend, he pulled it back out, "smiled," and went on to say, "In terms you will understand: basically time as you know it was suspended for three days on November 9, 2009, and every being was given the choice to stay with the planet or leave. Those who were unclear or close to the margin were assisted in their decision."

Further information was given to me that basically said that the planet was evolving, actually moving into a new space, a new dimension. Those that were ready would be making that change with her, but those who were not ready would be leaving as it would not be possible for them to stay. Again, he reminded me of the different levels of vibration and how positive and negative energy could not share the same space.

Da and his gang continued to show up for several more weeks. What he told me was that they were working to "raise my vibration" so that it would be more aligned with the new earth.

When I asked what the purpose of that was, he replied that it was so I could be of more assistance.

At the time I didn't have a clue as to what he could possibly mean by that.

Da stated, "There will be chaos and confusion as the vibration of the planet intensifies. Those that are not in alignment with the higher frequencies will suffer as the old falls away to make room for the new."

The physical symptoms brought on by the raising of my vibration were pretty intense, and I underwent a fair amount of discomfort, but I'd learned to trust in whatever I had gotten myself into with these higher dimensional beings. I'd made the decision to trust Da and not question his motives ever again— or so I thought.

Reminder from Da

The activity was very intense during this period of time, and it was only a week or so later that I had a disturbing interaction with them. As had been the pattern of late, it was the middle of the night, and I was aware of their presence in the bedroom. I felt them working with me while they had me in an altered state.

Da explained they were once again adjusting the level of my vibration.

I was communicating with him more in my mind, but I could also hear myself mumbling some words out loud.

My partner was beside me and later told me he could make out some of what I was saying, so he had an idea of what was going on but was not able to come fully conscious.

Eventually, they completed their task, and I came wide awake as did my partner.

I thought my session with them was over, but then I heard Da say that he had a message for me, and I needed to go over to my computer in order to see it. My laptop was shut down and sitting on an ottoman in the alcove off my bedroom.

His message didn't make sense to me. Besides, I was so tired I could barely move, and I must admit the idea of getting up was not appealing. I was out of whatever state I'd been kept in while they did their work, but now being fully awake, the idea of walking through my darkened bedroom while there were extra-terrestrial beings there did kind of frighten me.

So I firmly stated, "No, I'm not getting out of bed to read your message. Just tell me what it is."

Again, he said that I needed to go look at the computer screen.

I thought, *Is this a joke?*

I wearily but firmly said, "No."

And immediately up on the ceiling above the bed, there appeared a blue screen much like a computer or TV. It was about 18 or 20 inches square, and in the middle of the bright blue light was the black outlined image of an alien head. The eyes were their's as was the shape.

I asked my partner if he saw it and, of course, he did. I asked him if he knew what it was, and he replied that it was the head of a Grey alien.

We both lay in bed, looking at it for perhaps a half minute.

I was starting to get upset. I don't know if I was more angry with them or afraid. I'd felt relatively safe even though I was fully aware that I was communicating with extraterrestrials, but now I was starting to lose it. I wanted it gone, and I cried out for my mate to do something about it.

"Make it go away," I whined.

Quickly, he jumped up out of bed and went into the alcove and slammed the computer lid down. Oddly enough, doing that made the image disappear.

Later, when I asked him how he knew to do that, he didn't really have an answer. Neither of us recalled if the computer had come back on and had a blue screen or if it was still black.

A few nights later we tried to reenact the scene. We didn't get very far. It was ridiculous to even try. There was just no way possible for a computer, or any light for that matter, to be in that alcove and project onto the ceiling and show an image such as we'd observed. It just wasn't possible. There are half walls with pillars and a floor lamp in the way, but even so, a light would not project onto the ceiling from that room and give that kind of distinct image.

For several weeks after this episode, I was pissed—really mad at them for pulling such an adolescent stunt. From my perspective, I had met them more than halfway by remaining calm, and I'd been pretty proud of that achievement. For them to purposely scare me seemed ridiculous, childish, and out of line with the seriousness of what we were doing.

I didn't get an answer as to what it was all about until more than a year later. Around Christmas of 2011, they returned and I had the opportunity to ask Da about it. Here's how that exchange went.

Me: "So why'd you do that?" (Referring to the image on my bedroom ceiling)

Da: "Photo-op."

Me: "Photo-op? Photo-op? What—oh, for the book! Damn, you're right! That would have been awesome. Geesh, why didn't I think of that? My phone was right there! Damn, that woulda been great. Give me another chance, ok?"

Da: (amused) "Maybe. Actually that was not the purpose."

Me: "Really? So what was it all about?"

Da: "You have a tendency to talk yourself out of these experiences. You convince yourself that they are not real. We need you to understand this *is* real. We really have been here working to help raise your vibration, and the shift for humanity *really* is happening. This is not a dream. So we showed ourselves to you in the best way we knew how without creating panic in you."

Me: "Got it. Makes sense. Can you do it again though, so I can get a picture for the book?"

Da: "Are you sure you can handle the fear? We see you are alone."

Me: "I don't know—I will try."

Da: "We will see. You don't remember to take pictures when you see our ships."

Me: "But that's not fear. That's excitement. Maybe you could help by reminding me to take the picture."

Da: "Consider this your reminder."

The information that came out of that conversation was a real eye-opener for me. I'd been walking around feeling quite perturbed and justified about my anger. I'd viewed it from my perspective—a perspective that was still being perceived through a veil of fear, albeit a thinner veil, but it was still enough to distort and color the experience.

Once again, the lesson hit home with me. Nothing seen through the eyes of high emotion, especially fear, would be seen clearly. It simply is not possible. The rationale that Da gave made sense to me. The explanation was not one I could ever have come up with on my own. It was so far removed from what I'd been thinking that I would never have hit on such a thing.

He was right. If I'd not seen that image on my ceiling and not had the added confirmation of someone else seeing it, I would have convinced myself that all that "raising my vibration while in an altered state" was nothing more than a dream. Even though I'd been experiencing physical symptoms during the whole period of time it was going on.

Toto, I don't think we're in Kansas anymore.

Dorothy (*The Wizard of Oz*)

Chapter 12:
Awaking from the Dream

Active Participation with the Greys—Winter 2011

The sojourn each winter in Arizona had become a ritual for me, and the year of 2011 was no exception. What is it about the desert that has the power to transform and renew a person? It had taken me at least three years to fully appreciate the beauty that was present in the barren expanse of cactus and sand. Now I no longer saw a brown lifeless stretch of landscape but a magnificent bounty of vitality and aliveness. I walked the desert daily for miles and miles while I practiced silencing my mind through presence. I learned to turn away from the chattering nonsensical noise that was my ego and tune into the peaceful stillness of spirit.

I was awakening from the unconscious state where I'd spent the major portion of my life. As I re-established my relationship with my Creator, I slowly began to remember the truth of who I was. I continued my daily practice of surrender and allowed my life to be directed by the calm, loving energy of my Higher Self. The more I practiced this way of life, the easier it became, and I observed how effortlessly events and synchronicities showed up to direct me to exactly the right experience I needed in order to continue my growth and awakening.

During this time Da and his gang came back into my life with a vengeance. I was very grateful that I didn't have a job to be at every morning as I needed to be able to sleep in or take naps when the activity got intense. There were many days when I felt the exhaustion and wear on me from bouncing between the two lives I was living. My life had always had an odd quality to it, but now it became surreal.

The interaction with the Greys had shifted a great deal from what I'd experienced in the late 1980's. I was now an active participant and experienced virtually no fear. My contact with them was almost constant through the winter and spring of 2011/2012, and I was asking for clearer understanding of what was going on. I didn't get why I needed to spend so much time with them in their vibration and away from what I'd started to think of as my earth life.

As was true of pretty much all my requests, they supplied an answer. I had long ago come to the understanding that I was not a victim but a willing participant in some sort of program. The memory of this program was coming clearer and clearer each day, and it fascinated me. I knew without a doubt that I'd agreed to come into form on planet earth in order to be of assistance to her during this critical time in her evolution.

Nothing other than giving birth to my daughters even came close to how this felt—to learn the reason why I was here and to finally understand why I'd had such intense ET contact throughout my life. It was a huge relief, and it all made sense. Once I knew it, it felt as if I'd known it my whole life. *How could I not have connected the dots earlier?*

It was all so amazingly clear to me. I could only surmise that I was not meant to learn this until this particular time. As with everything else pertaining to this subject, it had all been planned quite well from the beginning, and I would learn what I needed to know *when* I needed to know and not before.

I realized that my abductions had served multiple purposes. One of the primary reasons for so much contact had been to keep my body healthy and safe—hence all the exams and seemingly invasive procedures. Another was about keeping my connection to them intact—that is, allowing me relief from the density of this planet's vibration while monitoring my general well-being and thereby explaining why Da's first question was always, "Sherry, are you happy"?

The harshness of this world was jarring, and it had not been an easy adjustment for me. They were not allowed to tell me the truth of what was going on, but they did try to subtly remind me of my mission and keep my focus on the role I was meant to play through their teachings and lessons. Knowing full well that I was displaying signs of grandiosity and fantasy, I could not deny that I finally knew the truth of my lifetime involvement with these guys. *They were my family.*

This new revelation was not easily embraced by me. I felt in my gut it was true. I absolutely *knew* it, yet it was so bizarre that the rational side of my mind wanted to argue and debate the issue.

Meeting My Hybrid Children

Then a funny thing happened. I started to experience a deep longing for that life—that is, the life I knew I was living when not focused in this world. And so I decided to ask a favor. I wanted to have a conscious meeting with my children—that is, my hybrid children. I knew I had quite a few offsprings, born from the ova Da had taken from me over the years.

To my utter amazement, my request was granted. Within a few days I was taken to what appeared to be a farmstead complete with a magnificent white two story house and outbuildings set in green rolling hills. It looked a lot like Wisconsin. I was led out onto a beautifully manicured expanse of green pasture that stretched out in front of me a good long distance. I was told to stand in a certain spot facing down the valley. There were steep, high hills off to my left covered in emerald green plants and a variety of strange foliage. To my right stood the farmstead, several small groups of people and tall, magnificent trees.

In front and behind me, I could see them bringing other humans out—most were female, but there were a few men in the mix. I would estimate there were about three dozen of us standing out in that pasture, all facing the same direction—

lined up one behind the other with a distance of about 30 feet between us. They then proceeded to do a fly-over. I was told that this was being done as a tribute to those of us who had actively participated in the hybrid program and gone "behind the veil" in order to serve the greater good, so this honor was not just for me but also for the others who had contributed in a similar fashion.

The ships were the small shiny, silver ones that were no more than twenty feet in circumference. There were hundreds of them, and they came in from all directions and converged together at the far end of the valley behind me. I watched in wonder as they came into single line formation and flew over our heads—very low, very fast, and oddly enough, on their side. It was an amazing spectacle, and it had a strong impact on me. This was their way of showing respect and gratitude, and I was hit with the knowledge of just how real this all was. The trauma I'd experienced, along with all the other "abductees," was being recognized, acknowledged and appreciated by them. It was then that I realized we'd all been part of something bigger and more meaningful than we'd ever imagined. It was mind-blowing and humbling--all at the same time.

After the fly-over I was taken to a two-tiered stone wall located in the huge grassy area in front of the house. There were about two dozen young adults sitting and milling about the wall. They appeared to range in age from about 16 to late 30s. I was told these were some of my children. It was an emotional moment for me, and I did feel as though I knew them but on a different level of awareness. Like so many other things to do with this subject, it is hard to explain.

Each one, in turn, stepped forward and embraced me as they re-introduced themselves to me. The prevailing emotion was one of love and respect. I would consider them all to be pretty normal-looking attractive humans with the exception of one young lady, who I would guess to be about age 30. She had a beautiful, bright light but was not a typical human. She apparently had another strong influence in her DNA that set her apart. They were all happy, engaging people; moreover, they were all of a vibration that is not found on planet earth.

There was more that occurred during this reunion, but I am not willing to share it. It's just too personal, but even so, there's a lot I cannot recall or was not allowed to retain, which is fine—anymore would have been overload. I was on a high for days after this took place, but initially my emotions were quite jumbled.

I never doubted the reality of the experience. I can understand you, the reader, doubting it. I believe I probably would if I were you, but it was definitely real, and the feelings I experienced took some time to sort out. I yearned to go back to that place but certainly was not ready to leave this world for good in order to do so. My emotions were a mixture of joy and sadness as I bounced between the love I felt for these beings and my deep longing to be with them. After all, they are my children—no matter what the circumstances of their birth.

This gift from Da helped to solidify the new perspective I'd recently gained. The fly-over tribute seemed to confirm for me the truth of my involvement in this program—I'd known before even coming here what my role would be. This explained a lot. I reflected back on all the times I'd begged Da to let me stay with him, as I'd felt more at home with him then I ever did here. And all the times I'd looked deep into my own eyes after having been in his presence—always searching for a clue as to the truth of who I was. Trying to remember what I'd known just moments before—before my memory was wiped clean.

Best of all, this newly acquired insight affirmed my belief that one is not able to be a victim. As if to give support to this new revelation, I soon came across an online video by author, lecturer, and teacher, Dolores Cannon that resonated so strongly with me, I knew it was no accident I'd stumbled upon it. I literally cried with relief to know I was not the only one thinking along these lines. I wasn't alone. There were millions of us who had volunteered to come to earth at this time to help with the birthing of the planet and humanity into the next phase of their evolution.

Growing Awareness of Humanity's Plight

As my awareness heightened, so did my understanding of humanity's plight. Where this knowingness came from, I cannot be certain, but it almost felt as if I were recalling an event or remembering a life I'd experienced before coming onto the planet. I could almost see myself in that other dimension, learning of Gaia's cry for assistance and knowing that I needed to respond. I, along with so many others had agreed to come into this dense three-dimensional world in an effort to bring humanity's vibration up from the dark place it had plummeted.

Planet earth is a living sentient being, and she had purposely held back her own ascension as she waited for her children to evolve to the point where they could make the journey with her into the higher frequencies. But over and over again, as earth humans reached the critical juncture, the fear so prevalent within them would cause a failure, and they would stay stuck in the three-dimensional vibration. It is an inviolate law of the Universe that you cannot interfere with another planet's development, so while the rest of the Universe continued on their journey of evolution, planet earth and her inhabitants were left behind to find their way.

Then in 1945 earth humans split the atom and created devastation, not only to their own planet but other dimensional realms as well, and the cry for help went out from Gaia to Source. Since the whole nature of creation is to experience itself and evolve, it is not surprising that the malicious behavior of those few humans caught the attention of our galactic neighbors. The Universe is a very structured and organized place—this kind of careless action could not be ignored. Humans were, once again, on a course of self-destruction—only this time, they weren't going to just put an end to their own evolution but destroy the planet as well. That would not and could not be allowed. Gaia was ready to move on—with or without her children.

The Diseased Body of God/Earth

In 2009 I'd been given a vision that supported this information. I was sitting on my bed looking out the window and really thinking of nothing when I felt as if I was lifted up very swiftly out of my body and sent hurling out into the cosmos. It happened very, very fast and in a matter of a few seconds, I was out beyond the stars and looking down at our Universe.

It was in the abstract shape of a man. There was deep, deep stillness and a profound silence that moved me beyond words. I knew I was in eternity—that is, timelessness, and I could very happily have stayed there forever. The peace and love was pervasive.

Then suddenly a gentle voice said, "This is the body of God."

Before I had time to even consider what I'd been told, I was rushing back down toward those stars and planets until I recognized our home—earth. It was located in the left thigh of what I'd been told was the body of God. As we came closer and closer to it, I was able to discern that this little cell, our earth, which made up a part of the whole was not a healthy cell. It was diseased.

The voice said, "She is sick. She will shake them off if she has to."

And I observed the cancer that was humanity.

"Do you understand?"

Then—plunk!—I was back in my bedroom and on my bed. It had all happened so fast. I was amazed and disturbed by the experience. The implication was clear. We, the human race, were like a parasite on the planet, destroying and infecting our home. She, the earth, is a living organism, and she has reached her limit. Humanity's time was about up. Either we wake up and realize what we are doing to each other and the planet, or we pay the consequences.

Planet Earth's decision to move into the 5th dimension presented a challenge for the humans residing upon her body. Most were not ready vibrationally to make that shift. But even so, the Creator decreed that it was time for his children of Earth to awaken. They'd been lost in their dream of separation long enough—but how to make that happen without direct interference from our galactic family?

A Call for Help

The powers that oversee the Universe decided that they would send in higher dimensional beings—that is, they would be born into human form in an effort to raise the consciousness of the planet. And so the call went out from the Galactic Federation of Light asking for volunteers. It was an aggressive, bold plan. The thing about the planet earth experience is that not only are you stepping into one of the lower vibrational systems, but it is a world quite unlike any other.

You see, on planet earth, the human species had fallen so far into fear that they had forgotten their connection to Source. They had forgotten they were one with their Creator, and so they'd become trapped in a cycle of rebirth and death. This world had something different from all the other planets— karma. In order to experience karma, one must come in with a veil of forgetfulness firmly in place. Without connection to Source, you quickly start to believe you are a body. You no longer know the truth of who you are—that is, an eternal being playing in form. Instead, you feel alone and abandoned.

It was not always this way on planet earth. Originally the first humans lived long lives of 700 to a 1,000 years in total awareness of their connection to Source. They understood the truth of who they were, and so their bodies didn't get sick or die. They lived in unity consciousness—in oneness. When they felt their spirit had learned all it could in this dimension, they simply put the body aside and ascended to the next level. This utopia went on for some time with planet earth being one of the most beautiful and loving places in the universe.

Devolution of Earth Beings

Then there came a time when Gaia volunteered to accept some lesser vibrational beings who had failed to evolve with the rest of their race. Their planet and the majority of the inhabitants were ascending into the next dimension, but these souls were not yet ready to move up the ladder. Out of compassion and love, planet earth and her children agreed to take these wayward, lost souls, believing that the love and light so prevalent here would awaken them, thereby making ascension possible for them.

Unfortunately, that is not what happened. Instead these denser beings brought havoc onto the planet. They brought with them the idea of separation, which produced guilt. Instead of living in the light, aware of their connection to the Creator, humans began to feel fear as they started to believe they were a body. They quickly began to devolve. These lower vibrational beings have stayed on planet earth causing much pain and suffering for the original gentle souls that were here. What's more, having the vibrational frequency of the planet drop to such a low frequency attracted other low vibrational beings to the earth. Gaia and her children stopped evolving and were left languishing in the third dimensional state for eons longer than was originally intended.

Earth humans have made several attempts to evolve into the 5th dimension, but each time all but a few failed to ascend. There are those residing on the planet who've have a vested interest in seeing earth and her children remain in the denser dimension. These controlling forces will not be able to stop the planet from ascending; however, they can have an impact on the humans. Those who do not go with the planet will not be lost forever—all will ascend eventually. It cannot be otherwise; at our core we are all eternal children of God, created in love.

We cannot die but we can take time—lots of time—getting to where we want and will get eventually. That is our free will—to stay in third dimensional reality or move into the 5th dimension.

My only question to you is "Why? Why would anyone choose to stay in this world of pain and separation?"

The volunteers began showing up on earth in the late 1940s. Many didn't stay long. The density of the human body, along with the fear-based thought system so prevalent, was just too much for these souls who were used to living in awareness. According to the rules of the game, we all had to forget the truth of why we were here and even forget our connection to God. It was very painful. We experienced major sadness, felt overwhelmingly homesick and were genuinely frightened of the human species. War, greed, violence, and domination over others were new experiences for us—and we didn't like it one bit.

I remember, as a very small child, looking at my body and wondering how I could take it off. It didn't fit well with me to be so contained within such a small, dense form. It was so limiting. I likened the human body to a coat or heavy garment. It didn't feel natural to me, but soon I, too, began to believe that that was who and what I was. I all but forgot my connection to Source.

And that is why I needed to spend so much time with Da—so I wouldn't experience a total disconnect. Being born onto planet earth and living in this society softened my image of the humans and made me so much more compassionate toward them and the overwhelming challenge they faced in awakening. At their core humans are amazingly loving and compassionate beings, but they have been imprisoned in this low density for so long it is no wonder they have forgotten who they are. It is no wonder so many do not even realize that now is the time to awaken. They are lost in their dreams of separation and fear.

Awakening to Our Innate Heart-Centeredness

So what does it mean to awaken? I think by now it is clear that it means to remember the truth of who you are. But more than that, it is living that truth by becoming heart-centered beings. It also means coming into awareness about what is going on around you—that is, not being afraid to see the truth of how humans have been controlled and dominated. These will be challenging times as the deceit and lies perpetrated on us continue to come to the surface for us to look at and be healed.

We will be called upon to forgive without judgment those who took advantage of humanity through manipulation and power. We will need to remember that there is no such thing as a victim. Everyone here agreed to come into this world and play a part in a dual-based system. There can be no judgment of those who played the part of the tormentor. We are building a new earth—one of unity consciousness. Please accept the message given to us by Da. It was given in love to help us lift ourselves up out of the fear based world we've been co-creating.

The entire universe reveres and appreciates you for the lessons you have brought forth by your experiences on earth. Never again will a planet be allowed to fall so far into darkness. You are resilient beyond belief and amazingly innovative and creative. Those who observed your journey and watched with sadness as the fear overtook you, cheered as you pulled yourselves up time and time again. They are inspired by your perseverance, determination, courage and imagination. Soon earth humans will be rejoined with their cosmic family. They want you to know that you have been missed, they want you to know that you are loved, and they welcome you back into the light.

Epilogue:
The Forgotten Promise

My contact with Da continues to this day, but I have noticed that my experiences don't seem to be as physical as they once were. It appears I am with them on an astral level, leaving the body behind more often than not, which is fine with me. They are an integral part of what is happening on the planet at this time, so I don't expect their activity to decrease, and I look forward to the day when they can be amongst us without either of our species having to alter their vibration or, worse yet, experience fear. The people who are closest to me are aware of this contact and quite often share in some of the encounters or have their own contact. I am extremely grateful to my amazing friends for supporting me and helping to keep me grounded. And I am grateful to Da. I am not yet ready to share all that he has done to keep me sane and steady, but it has been miraculous.

Recently I had very serious doubts as to whether I should allow this book to be published or not. I was stopped dead in my tracks when my daughter told me that she and her sister were contemplating suing me in order to keep the book from being published. That tore me apart. I have no relationship at all with my oldest daughter and a tenuous one, at best, with my youngest, so when she told me what an embarrassment I was to her, it hit me hard.

She implored me to stop acting and talking so crazy, saying that I was making it impossible for her to live and work in this town. The voicemail message she left felt like blows to my stomach, and I was sent reeling. I understood her fears.

Certainly her response was one most people might have. Word was already getting out about the book and, according to her, the jokes were flying. Now, I have been blessed with indifference; that is, I do not define myself by what others think of me, but I understand that not everyone feels that way. My daughter, like most, is sensitive to other people's opinions of her.

I told my best friend I was going to give serious thought to pulling the plug on it all; stop the lectures, stop the book, stop it all and, as I put it, "Go back into the matrix."

He asked if I could really do that at this point. I stated that I had to give it serious consideration as the price I was paying was too high. I couldn't bear to lose contact with my youngest child also—it was just too much to ask of me.

My daughter left her message for me on Monday, May 13th, 2013, and that night I went to bed fairly certain of what my decision would be. I was going to scuttle it all—I was tired—so very tired. I felt as if I'd earned the right to retire from this "mission" I'd been on. I would consciously go back into the matrix—that is, I'd go back to playing the part of a "normal" person in order to salvage what I could of my life and my relationship with my daughter all the while remembering the truth of who I was. But I would restrain myself from talking about it and do my best to blend in with society.

That night Da paid me a visit. His message was straight forward—like he could ever be anything but direct!

"Had I forgotten the promise I made? Did I not remember the vow I'd taken?"

When I pointed out the situation with my daughters, he showed great compassion and love toward me but made it clear that my obligations were to the greater good rather than the few. He then showed me that to acquiesce to my daughter's demands would not benefit our relationship at all. She would eventually see it as me allowing myself to be controlled and view it as weakness. She would lose respect for me. The lesson for her would be to see me persevere even in the face of ridicule—to see me hold my ground despite the odds and despite the price.

When he left, he made a minor spectacle of himself as there was a brilliant flash of light, the now familiar ear splitting crack and the electrical charge that causes my electricity to surge and then go out. It was exactly 2 a.m., and I sat up in my bed, holding my Pookie and smiling at his antics.

I knew he did that to imprint it in my memory. He didn't want me to think I'd dreamed this conversation—I needed to know, as always, that this was real. This was no joke. **This was no imagined fantasy. This was my life.** And it's as real as any other person's life—come to think about it, it was even *more real* than the old life I'd lived as a real estate developer and business owner. That life now felt like the fake life.

So I moved forward with the publication of the book, knowing that it would not be embraced by everyone and knowing that there are those who will ridicule it and me. But whether you believe the story or not is really none of my business or concern. The truth appears to be that I have been programmed to write this book at this particular time in humanity's development and whoever is meant to find the book and read it, will.

I have shared with you the secrets of my life—not an easy thing for a private person such as myself to do. The hope is that you will learn from my experiences. I began this journey believing I was the ultimate victim, and I ended it in a place of profound peace. How is that possible? How does one make the transition from overwhelming fear into complete peace?

As I referenced more than once, I found all the answers I sought in *A Course in Miracles*. The Course taught me that it is not possible to be a victim, and it answered one of my greatest, most pressing questions: Where was God in all this? I could never have come to terms with all that occurred and continues to occur in my life without the *Course*. Perhaps, best of all, the teachings in *A Course in Miracles* fall right in line with what Da taught me. It was very affirming.

Allowing peace into your life is by far the greatest gift you can give yourself, and that is the gift I am extending to you through the telling of my story. It is not a story of fear and pain but rather the overcoming of an anomaly that threatened to shake the foundation right out from under me. It is the story of love trumping fear. By transcending my fear, I was able to really hear what my seeming captors were teaching me and see these encounters for what they really were: a gift. A gift that forced me to view life from a higher, clearer perspective, and only by doing so would I learn the truth of who I was and why I was here.

It is my hope that you seek to find your own answers to the questions we should all be asking at this time in our evolution. What resonated with me may not work for you, but I do believe it starts with the understanding of the duality of the mind of man and the knowingness that we are so much more than this little life on planet earth would have us believe. For me, the surrendering of the ego and alignment of my will with the Divine was essential to the attainment of peace. I know that most people of earth cherish their free will, so when I speak about surrender and aligning my will with the Creator's, that might cause some unease in you.

I think the very label "free will" is quite misleading. It should be called *living in alignment with ego*—that is, letting that part of you that does not have your best interest at heart call the shots. So long as you cherish your "free will" and continue to direct your life according to that voice (the ego), you will find yourself in pain because you are essentially going against the truth of who you are. In surrendering your will, you are not really giving your power to someone else as was taught to us. Instead, we are one with God, so we are aligning with that part of ourselves that loves us unconditionally. Now doesn't it make more sense to live in step with *that* part of ourselves rather than the part that is based in fear?

As mankind moves through these next few challenging years, there will be much confusion as the old makes way for the new paradigm. You will be forced to look at your fears and release them through love, both on a personal level and as a society. The principles put forth in this book were given in an attempt to help you on this journey. My guys, known to you as the Greys, have a deep abundance of love for this planet and her children. They want you to know that. They have done and will continue to do all they can to assist in the transition, but they are not allowed to interfere—not that they would if they could. Interference would only set humanity back. This is your soul's journey. No one can make that trip for you, and you wouldn't want that to happen.

So I invite you to go in search of your own truth. And enjoy the adventure. It's amazing! I caution you to remember that the answers will not be found through analyzing, overthinking, or absorbing information. No, they are simple. The cliché is true: the answers are found within. They were there all along. They are found in stillness. What's so very beautiful about this is that for every person who awakens, it has the wonderful effect of pulling all of humanity's vibration higher. As was pointed out by Da when I was just a little girl—*"It starts with one."*

Namaste.

About the Author

Sherry Wilde

Sherry was born and raised in southwestern Wisconsin and continues to spend her summers there. She was a successful real estate broker, land developer and commercial renovator for over 25 years. You can connect with Sherry through her website at www.TheForgottenPromise.net.

Timeline

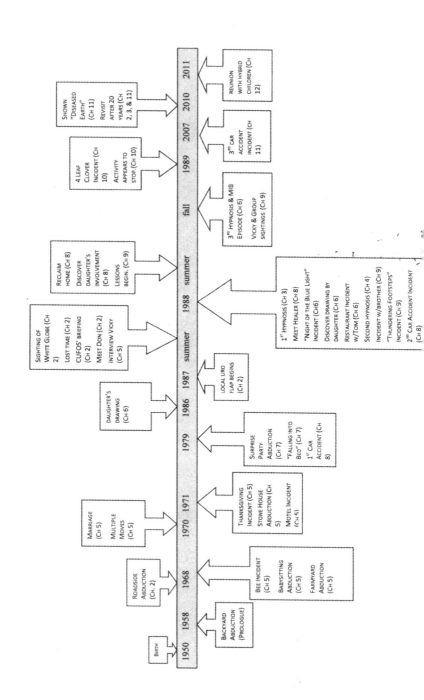

Other Books By Ozark Mountain Publishing, Inc.

Dolores Cannon
Conversations with Nostradamus,
     Volume I, II, III
Jesus and the Essenes
They Walked with Jesus
Between Death and Life
A Soul Remembers Hiroshima
Keepers of the Garden.
The Legend of Starcrash
The Custodians
The Convoluted Universe - Book One,
     Two, Three, Four
Five Lives Remembered
The Three Waves of Volunteers and the
     New Earth
Stuart Wilson & Joanna Prentis
The Essenes - Children of the Light
Power of the Magdalene
Beyond Limitations
Atlantis and the New Consciousness
The Magdalene Version
O.T. Bonnett, M.D./Greg Satre
Reincarnation: The View from Eternity
What I Learned After Medical School
Why Healing Happens
M. Don Schorn
Elder Gods of Antiquity
Legacy of the Elder Gods
Gardens of the Elder Gods
Reincarnation...Stepping Stones of Life
Aron Abrahamsen
Holiday in Heaven
Out of the Archives – Earth Changes
Sherri Cortland
Windows of Opportunity
Raising Our Vibrations for the New Age
The Spiritual Toolbox
Michael Dennis
Morning Coffee with God
God's Many Mansions
Nikki Pattillo
Children of the Stars
A Spiritual Evolution
Rev. Grant H. Pealer
Worlds Beyond Death
A Funny Thing Happened on the Way to
     Heaven
Maiya & Geoff Gray-Cobb
Angels - The Guardians of Your Destiny
Maiya Gray-Cobb
Seeds of the Soul
Sture Lönnerstrand
I Have Lived Before
Arun & Sunanda Gandhi
The Forgotten Woman
Claire Doyle Beland
Luck Doesn't Happen by Chance

James H. Kent
Past Life Memories As A Confederate
     Soldier
Dorothy Leon
Is Jehovah An E.T
Justine Alessi & M. E. McMillan
Rebirth of the Oracle
Donald L. Hicks
The Divinity Factor
Christine Ramos, RN
A Journey Into Being
Mary Letorney
Discover The Universe Within You
Debra Rayburn
Let's Get Natural With Herbs
Jodi Felice
The Enchanted Garden
Susan Mack & Natalia Krawetz
My Teachers Wear Fur Coats
Ronald Chapman
Seeing True
Rev. Keith Bender
The Despiritualized Church
Vara Humphreys
The Science of Knowledge
Karen Peebles
The Other Side of Suicide
Antoinette Lee Howard
Journey Through Fear
Julia Hanson
Awakening To Your Creation
Irene Lucas
Thirty Miracles in Thirty Days
Mandeep Khera
Why?
Robert Winterhalter
The Healing Christ
James Wawro
Ask Your Inner Voice
Tom Arbino
You Were Destined to be Together
Maureen McGill & Nola Davis
Live From the Other Side
Anita Holmes
TWIDDERS
Walter Pullen
Evolution of the Spirit
Cinnamon Crow
Teen Oracle
Chakra Zodiac Healing Oracle
Jack Churchward
Lifting the Veil on the Lost Continent of
     Mu

For more information about any of the above titles, soon to be released titles,
or other items in our catalog, write or visit our website:
PO Box 754, Huntsville, AR 72740
www.ozarkmt.com

Other Books By Ozark Mountain Publishing, Inc.

Guy Needler
The History of God
Beyond the Source – Book 1,2
Dee Wallace/Jarred Hewett
The Big E
Dee Wallace
Conscious Creation
Natalie Sudman
Application of Impossible Things
Henry Michaelson
And Jesus Said – A Conversation
Victoria Pendragon
SleepMagic
Riet Okken
The Liberating Power of Emotions
Janie Wells
Payment for Passage
Dennis Wheatley/ Maria Wheatley
The Essential Dowsing Guide
Dennis Milner
Kosmos
Garnet Schulhauser
Dancing on a Stamp
Julia Cannon
Soul Speak – The Language of Your
    Body
Charmian Redwood
Coming Home to Lemuria
Kathryn Andries
Soul Choices – 6 Paths to Find Your Life
    Purpose

For more information about any of the above titles, soon to be released titles,
or other items in our catalog, write or visit our website:
PO Box 754, Huntsville, AR 72740
www.ozarkmt.com